I Am Not an
ATM Machine

How Parents
Can Regain Control of Their Lives
While Still Loving
Their Children

Phil Clavel

Véhicule Press

Special thanks to Viviane Croubalian, Meghan, Zachary, Jordan and Michael, Pierre and Jacqueline, Simon Dardick, Vicki Marcok, Tim Thomas, Jim Hendry, Dave Liebman, Dr. Le, Lorraine Gerald, and Mary Clementoni.

Véhicule Press acknowledges the support of the Book Publishing Industry Development Program of the Department of Canadian Heritage and the Société de développement des entreprises culturelles du Québec (SODEC).

Cover design: David Drummond
Set in Minion and Gill Sans by Simon Garamond
Printed by Marquis Book Printing Inc.

LIBRARY AND ARCHIVES CANADA CATALOGUING
IN PUBLICATION DATA

Clavel, Phil
I am not an ATM machine : how parents can regain control
of their lives while still loving their children / Phil Clavel.

ISBN 1-55065-219-2

1. Adult children living with parents.
2. Parent and adult child. 3. Parents—
Finance, Personal. I. Title.
HQ755.86.C54 2006   646.7'8085   C2006-902379-4

Published by Véhicule Press, Montréal, Québec, Canada
www.vehiculepress.com

Distribution in Canada by LitDistCo
orders@litdistco.ca

Distributed in the U.S. by Independent Publishers Group
www.ipgbook.com

Printed in Canada on ancient-forest-friendly paper.

Contents

Thanks to Roger and Eve
for saying no just often enough.

Introduction

The unconditional love we give to our children is the very thing that makes it difficult to say "no" to them. One afternoon I was sitting with a group of parents who were also educators. Most of the parents who had children in their late teens or early twenties were bemoaning the extravagant expenses these children had accrued in the past few months.

A young mother of two toddlers was sitting at the table and said, "You mean this isn't the toughest age to deal with?" All the parents with the older children assured her in unison that it certainly wasn't. It became very clear that those of us with children in this age bracket were struggling to keep our heads above water financially, and a large part of that financial burden could be attributed to the financial demands that our children were placing on us. The biggest question we all sadly laughed about was, "How did we let it get to this?" None of us had the answer, but I decided to look at the phenomenon and come up with some tools parents could use to help them grapple with the problem.

I'm the father of two children and the step-father of two more. In addition, I've worked with teenagers for years. I'm amazed at the need they have to buy every gadget that comes on the market. When it comes to clothes they know all the designer labels. The only thing I knew about clothes at their age was that I preferred to buy Levis' jeans. Many of the unnecessary toys they surround themselves with are perceived as being absolutely necessary. However, the cost of these toys has become increasingly burdensome. I believe I am not alone in my attempts to deal with my children. Probably millions of parents are sacrificing a better quality of life to provide their children with these "status" items.

As a teacher I also noticed that grandparents had become increasingly involved with the raising of their grandchildren. I wondered if this practice was somehow related to the discussion that these parents had on that afternoon. Were children of varied ages downloading their expenses and responsibilities onto their parents regardless of age? I found examples that supported the theory immediately.

With that in mind I've written this book for parents of all ages. These pages will tell stories for parents attempting to deal with children who keep pushing both expenses and responsibilities onto them. These are children that have bought into the "play now, pay later" philosophy on the backs of their parents' income and love. It doesn't matter whether you are working class, middle class, wealthy, or a pensioner. If you have children who have adopted this philosophy, chances are you are going to be taxed by your children in one form or another. There are those children who may put this burden on you purely by accident, learn their lesson, and not ask you for anything else again. However, there are others that keep coming back to the trough for more. They cannot accept "no" for an answer and parents are left cleaning up after them time and time again. Then parents are left struggling with the emotional drain of having to say "no" to the very ones they want to please beyond anything else.

Over Indulgence

It's no surprise that many parents today feel held hostage to the demands of their children. Although we seem to fall into this trap when they are young, the demands become much greater as they get older. How many of us have over-indulged our young children at birthdays, Christmas, and other special events when we really couldn't afford to? To make matters worse, our children would never have missed the items that were not purchased! As these young children grow into their teens and beyond, their wants increase and so does the cost.

Society puts tremendous pressure on us to provide for our children, and fortunately the majority of parents take on that responsibility quite happily. Perhaps by accident, possibly because of the times we live in, many of us are not able to differentiate between what our children want and what they actually need. Parents place themselves in perilous financial situations so their child has the best designer clothes or so they can drive a fancy sports car.

How many parents are trying to save money to retire or have a vacation, or possibly buy some new clothes for work, while their son or daughter is in their twenties, staying at their house rent-free, eating their food and having all services provided for free? This minimum wage freeloader could be driving a fancy car and blowing a single paycheque on a designer shirt to look good at the club that night. By the way, they'll need to borrow $40.00 to go out!

Play Now Pay Later

Baby boomers grew up in an era where we received the message from our parents that we would be able to improve our lifestyle beyond our parents'—if we had the initiative.

Are our children taking so much from us because they realize they won't be able to live in the same lifestyle that we have become accustomed to? Their "grab and play" lifestyle appears to have little regard for the future despite the fact that many of them are continuing their education at the same time.

Boomers are not immune to the "play now, pay later" phenomenon. Many have taxed their parents' patience by constantly showing up at their door looking for handouts. It's not unusual for parents in their seventies and eighties to be asked to pay for the mistakes of their sons and daughters who are well into their fifties and even sixties. Often they have become full-fledged parents again when the expense of raising their grandchildren has fallen right into their laps.

A large number of children of all ages believe a message that our society continues to give them. That message is that they deserve better and society owes them. They have developed a selfish attitude that targets the people who love them the most, their parents. Parents are often under tremendous pressure and feelings of guilt to provide things for these children that they don't need. The crazy thing is that the parents themselves put their own financial security at risk to provide for these nonsensical wants.

The "play now, pay later" phenomenon is not tied to economic status. Children of working class parents are just as likely to be tempted by society's bombardment of "perceived needs" as are children of more wealthy parents. The biggest difference is the cost of the toys they are asking for. The result is that these wants can be burdensome on any family regardless of income. Remember, many children have the perception that they are owed these things, so why should they set limits on what they want?

Of course, there have always been large numbers of people who wanted more than they could actually afford. The biggest difference between those people and the offspring who I am referring to in the twenty-first century is that these children have little regard for the cost and, in particular, who is going to pay for everything. Unfortunately, it is the parents who are faced with these bills on a regular basis when they had nothing to do with purchasing or enjoying the service or items. How many parents out there have had to cancel their teenager's cell phone?

Values

The Great American Dream was built on the basis of specific values. Most can be found in Horatio Alger's "rags to riches" stories from the mid-to-late nineteenth century about homeless boys growing up in New York City. However, the foundation of his stories was always based on a set of very simple values. His message was that if you worked and studied hard over a long period of time, showed honesty, avoided vices, and had a little bit of luck, the opportunities were limitless. Many people in our society no longer hold these values. They've lost hope, or believe they can't possibly attain the lofty goals either they or their parents have set for them.

Values have become much more difficult to pin down in our society. The family is not the same as it once was. Divorce and two income families have seriously limited the time that families actually spend together. The lure of new technologies such as the Internet has become a much too familiar place to many children of all ages. Remember, we are all someone's child and you can be lonely at ten or at sixty. The Internet provides companionship and promotes values that are not monitored by society in general, or parents in particular. Combined with this is the rise of legal gambling. Children are exposed to it everyday on television and the Internet through poker tournaments or advertisements for websites.

The result of these changes is that many of our children want instant gratification. A personal computer in our hands now really means that if you push a button you get instant results. The result can become part of the lifestyle that many are living today. Young people and many adults today will tell you that they cannot go anywhere without their cell phone. They need to let people know what they are thinking or have others call them. It is not about how important the discussion is as much as it is about having the instantaneous feedback and reward. If you don't believe me, just try and have your teenager give you their cell phone for a few hours. It's not going to happen very easily!

1. Why am I in This Mess?

It is difficult to pinpoint when this transformation took hold, but it most obviously is rooted in the baby boomers' need to provide the very best for their children even though they may not be able to afford it. Boomers raised in the sixties were the first children exposed to the power of "credit" through their parents. This was the beginning of credit cards as we know them today. Credit cards gave access to many things that the average family had previously been denied. I clearly remember going to a department store with my parents in the late sixties and seeing a small stereo system that I really liked. My parents said that if I liked it, they would buy it, and I could pay for it monthly through their new credit card that they were given at the store. I knew right away that there was something wrong with this picture. My dad was a bus driver and my mom stayed home to look after me and my six brothers and sisters. My parents had never had money to buy any of us anything too extravagant, so this offer was a huge departure from that reality. It was such a huge departure that I still remember the offer some forty years later. I recalled having this reflection right in the store in front of my parents and the stereo. I decided not to take the stereo based on that reflection and out of fear that I would not be able to pay for it. I still have vivid memories of a steady stream of bill collectors coming to our home when I was growing up!

Evolving Parental Roles

When looking at social change over the last forty to fifty years, you cannot ignore the tremendous change that the role of the mother has experienced. In the fifties and sixties the pressure that came with the role was to be a good mother and housekeeper. This was my mother's role. Into the seventies and eighties the role evolved to where the mother was not only expected to be a good housekeeper but also a hard-working employee. In today's society the mother's role also includes that of maintaining her own personal identity. That may mean time out of the house with girlfriends, time at the gym, spa or esthetician, and time for personal interests. Obviously, this gradually meant less time available for the children.

As a result father's role needed to evolve as well. The father of the fifties and sixties was generally the main wage earner in the home. His contact with the children before and after work was there, but it had more to do with his presence. As mothers began to work outside the home, fathers were forced to take a more active role in child- rearing. Today, because of the fast-paced lives of both parents, fathers spend much more of their time sharing parental duties.

Coming from a large working class family and being a teenager through the sixties the difference between our "needs and wants" was very clear. As a large family we *needed* groceries in the house by each Saturday morning. As a family we expected this to happen and we celebrated that reality. We *wanted* to go out to the local family restaurant, but it was something we rarely could do. Mother's Day comes to mind as possibly the only time we ever did this, and I still don't know how my father could have afforded this. I *needed* a new pair of shoes to start school each year. I *wanted* other shoes during the year, but it was not part of my reality. I distinctly remember having to wear a pair of my father's shoes when I was twelve or thirteen to end the school year.

Our life then was very simple and focussed around shelter, food, and clothing. However, the family unit played a major role in who we were and the values we shared. As fragile as my family's financial situation might have been, there was an umbrella of protection there. Not that the family was one big happy group! It was, and still is, rarely that with so many siblings in it. We had many battles in that small three-bedroom duplex that we lived in for so many years. However, I believe each of us left home with a sense of family and caring for others.

Commercialism

My earliest memories of commercialism are centred around a few memorable items from the sixties. I remember people wanting bola bats and yoyos. I also remember the hula-hoop craze. I can recall using my own money to buy a very early version of the Frisbee. I had never seen one before but I bought it and it became a craze after. My older brother had Elvis records that I listened to when he wasn't around. This got me interested in records and when I was older this would be where my extra money would go. I still have that small record collection from the sixties. I had a paper route from the time I was in grade four, so I some-times had spending money my brothers and sisters didn't have.

Looking back, the biggest indicator of the commercial-ism that we now face in society was present in a very limited extent in the sixties. This was the age where Barbie dolls and GI Joes were created. We were swamped with items from the Beatles. There were Beatles posters, pins, wigs, cards, hats, and on and on the list of items went. Many of us had some of these items. Somehow, the "needs" that are expressed today by many of us and our children were born out of these "wants" from our yesterday. These items, and they can vary, trigger a moment or time that brings back fond memories for many boomers, even today.

As we moved into the seventies, many things changed in society that would affect us forever. Boomers moved out of their parents' homes and looked into starting out on their own. We were moving into the work force and would become the major market for anything we were interested in and even some things we weren't interested in but had been convinced we were. Eight-track tapes are a case in point. In many cases, our parents were right in terms of our potential for a better lifestyle. If we went after it, there was the distinct possibility that our lifestyle could surpass our parents'. At this point, we had more colour, fashion, and gadgets than our parents could ever have dreamed of when they were young.

Our parents had focussed on family after World War II. They tried to make a home and raise their kids. In the seventies, we treated ourselves, and if we accidentally had kids, we still treated ourselves. There was no avoiding the barrage of advertising that encouraged us to buy. At this point, you'd have had to be pretty down and out not to be able to get a credit card. Unlike our parents, you didn't have to be put through the third degree by a bank or credit card company to get one. Many of us had more than one card, and I'm not even talking about the department store credit cards.

Two-Income Family

However, the single biggest difference that the seventies heralded, in terms of family, was the two-income family. The two-income family would forever change the way we lived. At first it allowed us the opportunity to enjoy many of the things we had wanted when we were younger but didn't necessarily need. As we got more comfortable with this dual income we treated ourselves even more. We started buying two cars instead of one. Trips to more exotic destinations became more affordable. Our parents may never have been able to afford a trip to Hawaii, but that wouldn't stop us!

Throughout the late 1960s, 70s, and into the 80s there was a major shift in society's thinking in terms of women and education. Increasing numbers of women were entering colleges and universities. Some of these institutions had been exclusive to men well into the sixties. Women were now looking at many more options besides going to secretarial school, teaching, or entering the workforce right after high school.

The relatively easily available birth control pill also enabled women to be in school for a much longer period of time because they did not have to interrupt their schooling to start a family. Couples started having children at a later age and, unlike previous generations, in more and more couples each partner could have a university degree.

As women invested greater amounts of time in their education, they began to have careers they wanted to take much more seriously. The personal and financial rewards of a career were not roles that they were willing to give up. As a result, improved parental leave plans were established to allow women the opportunity to have children and then

21

return to the workforce.

Society was beginning to shift in its recognition of the valuable role women were playing in the workforce. When I started teaching in the mid-seventies many of the women I worked with saw their careers as secondary to their husbands', but within a few years, it was easy to see that women in teaching were seeing their careers as equally important as their spouse's career.

After society had made the shift towards accepting increasing numbers of women in the workplace, management had to take notice. It was no longer acceptable to promote only male managers when the workforce had as many or more female personnel equally qualified to occupy management positions. Slowly, women began to take their place in management positions on a regular basis.

As this shift progressed so did the increase in the number of daycares for the children of two-income families. For the first time in North American society young children were being raised, for long periods of time, outside the family home. Not only were children being raised by strangers in daycares, but they were also being exposed to a wide variety of other children without parental supervision.

Our children grew very comfortable with these new surroundings. After the initial anxiety of going to a new daycare, they quickly fit into this new daily routine. At times parental anxiety over daycare seemed to be much greater than the child's. My children went to two separate daycares and seemed to enjoy both.

How much control did we give up by spending less time with our children at such a young age? There is no easy answer. Our children began to socialize more outside of the family home at an earlier age. They were exposed to larger amounts of toys at the same time as we were. We compensated by spending more on anything that we thought would make our lives more efficient. Our children were often the recipients of these gifts. Being in a two-income family allowed us to enjoy more things with our families—but in a limited amount of time.

Extra Cash

Our entertainment budget increased dramatically. We went to movies more often. Discos blossomed all over the place, so we could hang out on the weekend. Rock concerts were the norm. We embraced bands like the Eagles, and to this day, even after taking "a thirteen year vacation" they grow more wealthy off of our loyalty. We began a tradition of treating ourselves if we pleased. Why wait for a better day when you could do it now!

Restaurants were having a field day with us. We were more than happy to go out and eat on a regular basis. There's a reason why McDonald's expanded at a tremendous rate during this period and sustained such profitability. We liked those burgers and we wanted them. We weren't thinking too much about health at that point. After all, in your twenties or thirties, you're not feeling that you are too vulnerable to health problems beyond family heredity issues. Lifestyles were changing and there was less time for cooking that family meal on a consistent basis. It was much easier to pay for some fast food than to prepare a meal after a long day at the factory or office. This would prove costly in the long run for a multitude of reasons, but who knew!

As we married, started families and moved into homes into the eighties, suburbs expanded and home sizes grew and offered more conveniences. Our children would be able to have their own rooms. There would be no need for them to share their living space. We could afford more for our families and our children would reap the fruits of our labour. As well, there would be lessons on everything: piano lessons, ballet, singing, acting, and lessons you couldn't imagine—also soccer, baseball, hockey, scouts, football, and any other organized activity you could imagine. Thank Detroit for the mini-van because now parents had the means to run wild through the suburbs with their screaming children. Suburban streets would never be safe again as these parents obsessed about making sure that their children kept to a tight schedule during their child's "free time".

The week-end as we knew it would never be the same. Whatever happened to Saturday morning groceries and Sunday night with Ed Sullivan and Bonanza?

Deprivation?

It's at this point that our love for our children appeared to become directly connected to our financial well-being. I should have been tipped off with the Cabbage Patch craze from the mid-eighties. I mean, really, who wanted those dolls anyway? Let's be honest, we did! We fell in love with them and so our kids had to have them. Have you ever heard anyone say they were deprived because they didn't get a Cabbage Patch doll?

I didn't think so, but this is where I started to hear about depriving our kids. And this so-called deprivation was directly linked to unnecessary items like Cabbage Patch dolls. We had those stampedes for Tickle Me Elmo much later. Then the obsession with Beanie Babies arrived. This was over-indulgence at its worst. You couldn't be a parent and go out shopping anymore and not be confronted with hundreds of these things everywhere. And god forbid if you had your children with you! There is no way you would get out of the store without dropping some extra dollars. Some parents actually believed this was an investment for their children. I know one couple who put themselves into debt collecting these things, thinking they were going to be an investment and increase in value for their children. Neither parent fought for ownership of the Beanie Babies during their divorce.

Kids today have to have Harry Potter books. Parents line up to make sure they get that new book as soon as the publisher releases it. And to create more unnecessary hype, why not release it at midnight to raise the anxiety level. Who would believe that parents actually lined up to buy these books? Maybe they were afraid that the publisher wouldn't want to make money anymore and would stop printing the book. I suspect it is more closely related to the deprivation I discussed earlier. As our children grew up so did their taste in toys. Beanie Babies are looking cheap compared to some of the gadgets that they are interested in today.

In summary, many of us gave our children the things we never could have dreamed about in our own youth. However that would be an over-simplification of what happened. Daycares, nannies, early school, and personal interest and preferences are an important dynamic in how we interact with our children. In fact, perhaps we were using these items to compensate for the very thing that we could not give them: time. As a result, the conclusion was that a child without these items was deprived. We were buying these items so our children would be comfortable when we were not there. As those times away from our children increased so did our guilt—and the unnecessary toys.

Key Points

- The use of credit has become rampant in society and children learn to manipulate that concept at a young age.
- Parental roles have evolved over the last decades so that the sharing of parental duties is more evenly divided.
- Two-income families have allowed families to have more funds to do things than at any earlier time.
- As a result of more disposable income, commercialism has reached an all-time high so that most items are hyped and over-advertised although they are often not necessary.
- Over-indulgence of children often begins at a young age because of a need to provide things.
- Often over-indulgence is used to compensate for less time being spent with children.

2. Society's Toys

I find interaction with teenage children to be very similar to transactions in other parts of my life. It's difficult to get a specific time from teenagers about when they are going to be home. You have to negotiate with them to have dinner together. It's a mediation session when attempting to get them to clean their rooms. Time together is often an intrusion on their personal life, and is usually clocked if it exists at all. So if you are successful in gaining their attention, you will have a limited amount of time with them.

We are the first people they turn to in a crisis. The underlying principle, however, is that you had better agree with their analysis of the crisis. If your opinion differs there is something wrong with you and your thought processes. They feel equipped to deal with all the pitfalls that life has to bring. The only problem with that philosophy is that it usually comes at a price. And, when the going gets tough, it is usually Mom and Dad who get stuck with the financial messes that they have created.

Fun Things Like iPods
My kids have never been afraid of work. They have all had a variety of part-time jobs over the years. As I have often pointed out to them, it is not how much you make, but how much you spend that determines your financial security. Young people today are a driving force in the life of the

urban and suburban mall. Not only are they staffing these multi-million dollar complexes, but they are doing it all on minimum wage. To further benefit the owners of these malls, the largely teenage staff then turn around and pump the money right back into the stores where they work. At one time my daughter had so many hooded sweatshirts they were taking over her bedroom.

With the bombardment of commercials that have introduced our children to every type of unnecessary item it is no wonder that they are an easy target to give up their cash. They need those MP3 players until iPods are more popular and then they'll need iPods. It was great when we bought a DVD player for the house, but by the time I did that, they wanted their own portable DVD player. And of course, there are portable computers and digital cameras.

The absolute must for kids of all ages is the cell phone. I remember buying a cell phone so I would be able to stay in touch with my kids. They use it to stay in touch with their friends! Their family is anyone with their cell phone number. It is rarely turned off and they are always on call. As much as I relish my down time away from work and enjoy peace at home, they fear it. They are uncomfortable with the thought of being disconnected from friends. Their phones have personalized ringers and a place of honour in strategic spots around the house so they can be heard from everywhere. They will not be deprived of the necessity to remain in contact with their friends at all hours. The cell phone is an essential part of their identity and they feel uneasy without it.

The Need for More
Our children are able to travel all over the world in minutes

via the Internet and many of them have been exposed to everything the Internet has to offer from a very young age.

They see more things more quickly than ever before and they often know what they are looking for. The dark side of this technology is that they can also be exposed to seedier parts of life than we would never knowingly allow into our homes. The reality is that it is in our homes and is available to them with a simple touch on a keyboard!

Over-indulgence of our children when they are young leads them to indulge themselves even more as they grow older. We continually reward mediocrity in our children, leaving them with the delusion that they are the best or superior in many ways. There is a reason why thousands of young people line up for a show like American Idol, seriously believing that they have what it takes to be a star. More later, on how we can avoid this fantasy world.

Many of the things that I am talking about are not restricted to our children's habits and attitudes. There are boomers who have been exposed to many of the same things over the years. For whatever reason, they have also grown more emotionally distant from their parents and yet are still quite dependent financially. They may be tapping into the pensions of their parents or chipping away at the inheritance. Some are even frustrated with the length of time it is taking for them to get their inheritance. These parents or grandparents are still maintaining a lifestyle in whole or in part for the children they gave birth to as much as sixty years earlier. Some might argue that it is a privilege to do this, but at what point is it no longer productive? How long does it take to become handicapped by this dependency? These are questions that need to be asked and answered regardless of your financial well-being.

Vices

Many parents have also ended up supporting habits or addictions that have taken over their children's lives. In an effort to feel the high of success that has eluded them, children of all ages turn to vices that bring ruin to many people, both emotionally and financially. Life today glorifies and makes readily available such things as prescription medications, on-line poker, casinos, and video lottery machines. Alcohol and illegal drug use can also get thrown into the mix. Any of these have the potential to create addicts out of our children. Parents of all ages are dealing with the fallout of these vices on a daily basis. It puts a huge strain on families and individuals.

Most of our children will jump on the roller-coaster ride of life, get through it very well and become independent and healthy young adults. Life will bring them an abundance of joy that will be transferred to us as their proud parents. As this ride is moving, however, it is important to be aware of the strategies that can be used to help them cope as adults. In addition, parents need to protect their financial assets so they can have a quality of life that they have worked towards for so many years.

This book will look at specific issues that parents have been dealing with and will continue to deal with in the future. Suggestions will be made for better practices when dealing with children—along with anecdotes from my own experiences. This is written as a guide for those parents who are searching for answers to problems that have been persistent while raising their own children, regardless of age. Some of you may use these suggestions: others may be motivated to try a different solution based on your own experiences combined with the ideas expressed here.

Key Points

- Teenagers are extremely difficult to pin down for even the most consistent of activities like dinner.
- Negotiations are common when attempting to get children to help out around the house.
- Many young people have part-time jobs and therefore a large discretionary income.
- Our children have a wide access to the rest of the world via the Internet.
- Most young children must stay connected to their friends and having grown up in the cell phone generation makes it possible.
- American Idol syndrome is an extension of the over-indulgence that children have experienced from a young age.
- Adult children are not immune to the idea of taking from their parents.
- Addictions are taxing not only to society but also to families.
- Parents of all ages need strategies to cope with the escalating demands of their children.

3. Preventative Medicine

I'm not sure there is any guaranteed way to bring up a child so that they don't become so self-absorbed that they have little regard for a parent's financial constraints. There are some helpful strategies to make your child more aware of everyone's responsibilities, including his or her own. From their birth children take their cues primarily from Mom and Dad and the rest of the immediate family. It is only later that the influences of the rest of society—including peers—begin to play a much more influential role. The groundwork established by you as the parent will go a long way towards helping your children develop into independent young adults.

A great story comes to mind about young children and their understanding of the value of money. A mother told me the tale of her boys watching the television and seeing something they both liked. They asked their mother if they could go to the store and buy this toy. Their mother explained to the boys that she didn't have enough money to buy what they wanted. The two seven-year-olds calmly replied, "Mom, all you have to do is go to that big machine where the money comes out!" Talk about a learning opportunity! She had taken the boys to the bank machine on many occasions and they had quickly learned that following the encounter with the machine, their mother purchased what they wanted. The behaviour had been established—

and the expectation. However, when you are a single mother with two little kids, it is only natural that you are going to do bank machine withdrawals with your kids present.

Teach Your Children Well

Our busy lives don't always allow us to conduct an analysis of specific activities like the bank machine incident. Yet there are some important things that we can learn from this. The first thing to remember is that when your paycheque is a direct deposit, your children never see money going into the bank machine. The child sees the interaction of the parent with the machine simply—buttons are pushed in order to extract cash. Once there is cash, the child is often rewarded. It is important that the parent educates the child about how money gets into the machine. Once the world of work is explained it is also important to describe the various things that the money from the machine has to be used for. A parent doesn't have to go into detail, but the concept of paying for food on the table, as well as shelter, electricity, phone, and clothing should somehow be connected. As a parent I took for granted that my kids understood this when they were little, but I'm not so sure that was the case.

Once you've established the relationship between what you earn, what is placed into the bank machine, and what comes out of the bank machine, children can also understand the concept of percentages. Children love working on puzzles and they can easily piece together the various percentages needed to pay monthly bills. Monthly billing can then be related to the expenses of the home. You could do this by actually creating your own puzzle that the children have coloured for you. The pieces could have words like "telephone" as well as a percentage number on each. Once

33

the puzzle is put together, it shows all the things that Mom and Dad have to take care of on a monthly basis. This does not have to be drilled into your child but you want him/her to be comfortable with the concepts. Do not harp on constant problems with paying bills. The exercise should be geared towards solutions. It is important not to raise the anxiety level of the child and specific dollar amounts need not be discussed. There is not a better way to teach math (let alone money concepts), than by using situations that have direct meaning in a child's world. Remember, sooner or later your child will grow up and need to effectively handle these same responsibilities. Why not give him/her an early education in life skills. Children are being exposed to gross commercialism at a very young age. It is important that parents also educate their children at a young age on how to deal with this assault.

Shopping Trip
Shopping is another critical time in a child's understanding of financial concepts that he/she will have to rely on later in life. As any parent knows, the trip to the store can turn into a nightmare should your child decide to have a tantrum over something they want. The tantrum is usually about what they are not allowed to have. Money is never part of the equation. It is always about the child wanting it then and there, or else. This is another situation where the groundwork has not been laid to prevent this type of outburst. The tantrum occurs because the child has learned to train his/her parents. Initially a trip to the store would have involved giving the child a small reward when it wasn't necessary. This could continue until the child is finally refused a request at the store by the parents. The child then

flies into a tantrum and the item lands in the shopping basket. The child and parents have changed the nature of the trip. Initially, it would have been a great time to spend quality family time together. At the point of the tantrum, it becomes an activity dreaded by the parents. The result is that parents then try to avoid bringing the child to the store—thus less family time is spent together. But what else could have been done to avoid the situation?

It's Difficult to say "NO"

It is extremely important that the child understand the importance of the word "no". It is also important that he/she understands that his/her parents mean it when they say it. The other thing is that the child must learn to appreciate the things that they have been given. The meaning of no must be reinforced in the home prior to engaging in a store-front battle. If a child has a good understanding of no then battles will be avoided.

How can a parent do this? The answer is simple, stop giving into requests when your initial response is no. By giving in to requests after an initial no, you have taught your child that no means absolutely nothing when you say it.

Some parents indulge their children in all kinds of things that are unnecessary. I'll never forget one of my first friends when I was about seven. Steven's dad used to walk from the train station each night with a bag of goodies that he bought for his son. I would be there when Steven would be rifling through the bags. He would be swearing at his father for not getting all the specific things he wanted. I would be witnessing this after coming from my home where there just wasn't anything extra like he was getting. His dad was buying miniature train pieces and silver dollars as well as chips and cokes. Coming from my background it was like another world, but I knew there was something wrong with the picture. Steven's father died when Steven was still in high school, and I could not help thinking that he never really appreciated everything his father had done for him.

As parents, when we say no to a child we often feel more badly than the child feels and so we often back down. Setting specific routines around bed-time, bath-time, and meal-time significantly increases your chances of being able to control your child beyond those key activities. If you are not able to say no in the privacy of your own home, you are never going to be able to do it in a toy store with other people around. Being able to control daily activities and provide guidelines and limits for behaviour enables a parent to maintain leverage with the child as he/she grows up. Your child will acknowledge the boundaries that have been established by complying with the guidelines. As our children grow older, it is this acknowledgement and compliance with our wishes that will help them deal with a world that continually bombards them with brash commercialism of the imaginable and sometimes unimaginable.

Be a Good Role Model

As parents we are role models for our children. Remember, the goal is to maintain a certain amount of control while giving your children the tools necessary to make educated decisions regarding financial commitments. Parents of all ages are subject to the same commercialism as everyone else. Restraint is the operative word when it comes to spending, no matter what your economic bracket is. Teaching your children that just because you can afford something does not necessarily mean that you need it, is invaluable, particularly once they start earning their own money. Shopping for bargains should be the norm rather than the exception. Getting full value for a fraction of the list price is something that should be celebrated. However, there are items that should be considered less frivolous and more important to the lifestyle of the individual family members. Teenagers will pick up on that point and argue their case in terms of need if they really want something. The key thing to always come back to is that spending must always be within their means. What financial responsibilities do they already have? This comes back to the puzzle activity I mentioned earlier that focussed on budgeting. It may sound silly to do this, but our children will all be inundated by credit card companies eager to put them in debt permanently if they can. I think it's fair that as parents we are able to do a little early childhood financial training.

Gift-Giving Time

Gift-giving is always a time when we come under tremendous scrutiny from our children. How we handle special times like birthdays, Christmas, Hanukkah, and other special events become benchmarks for our children. After all, these are the times when we are most vulnerable to over-indulging our children: if a sweet sixteen party costs $10,000, then what happens at twenty-one? A teenager who gets a new car for graduating from high school will expect something pretty spectacular when graduating from college. Obviously, these examples are at the upper economic range of gift-giving, but the percentages can snowball at any financial level. And that snowball effect can have a crippling effect on the financial well-being of parents.

One of the things that often happens around special

events like birthdays is that children receive a fair amount of cash from relatives like grandparents. Chances are if a parent does nothing about it, the child is going to turn around and spend as much as has been received. There is usually little thought to saving any part of this gift. Saving should be both encouraged and compulsory if cash gifts are received. Prior to the event it should be made clear to the child and the gift-givers that a portion of the money will be put away as savings. The exception could be if a child is saving for something in particular and that the item is valued by the parents—such as a school trip that would be an invaluable experience. My son went on a trip to England with his school band, but the criteria for him going was that he contribute a certain percentage of the total cost.

I remember friends of mine who would prepare gift lists for their two children months before Christmas. The gift lists were comprised of all the things that their children had asked for. The difference with these parents was that their children were going to get everything on the list. Family and friends were instructed about what to buy prior to Christmas. Once someone had committed to buying a specific gift, the gift was crossed off the list. The result was that the children got everything on the list. There was no compromise or choice to be made, and the parents did not teach that there were any limitations.

Developing the ability to make choices, particularly good ones, from an early age is an invaluable skill for a child to learn. When children grow up they will not be in a position to have everything they want. They need to develop the skills to make appropriate choices that will protect them from advertising that makes everything seem necessary. We can help children come to the realization that it is not possible to have every possible type of Barbie or computer toy, and it is absolutely not necessary. Overindulgence, in any part of their life, is unnecessary and wasteful. If this happens it will only increase as your children get older and you will be burdened with the cost.

Walk in These Shoes

When I was young and even when my kids were younger, shopping for a pair of shoes, particularly near the start of the school year, was a big event. I can't remember having my shoes picked out prior to going to the store, and I certainly wasn't going to determine how much was spent on the shoes. Today, the kids know all the different brands. They also know which brands are hip and which ones to avoid. They are not concerned about choosing a pair of running shoes that could run into the hundreds of dollars.

It is crucial to set the parameters for an excursion to buy something like a pair of running shoes prior to going to the store. You don't want to be in the middle of the store and find yourself looking for a running shoe mediator. Believe me, parents are often caught in this predicament, and often become so frustrated that they cave into the fashion pressure. It's too late to start the negotiation once you have seen the shoe of your teenager's dreams. You've already lost. To protect yourself, set the time and place you will be going shopping for the shoes as well as the amount that you are willing to spend.

This allows you to maintain control of this event. Your child's choice will be whether or not to shop within the parameters. If not then it means the loss of the new running shoes. This is a simple trip to the store that thirty years ago you wouldn't have had to think twice about. Today, if you're not careful with this shopping trip, you may have to borrow from your line of credit to be able to pay your rent at the end of the month.

Allowance

An allowance is a good way to help children understand the importance of saving and wise spending. By wise spending I mean using their money carefully to buy things that they would like to have but can also afford. By saving I mean being able to afford things that would otherwise be unattainable. As they grow older, children will eventually be in a position to take out all kinds of credit in order to purchase the things they want.

However, at a young age they only have one option as long as a relative doesn't interfere to finance a purchase. Yes, we shoot ourselves in the foot all the time! We are usually the first line of credit that these children have in their lives. Only our line of credit is special, they don't have to pay interest, and here's the kicker, they never have to pay us back!

Parents often debate the whole concept of allowance. Some parents simply state, "When you need money for something, come and ask me and then I'll give it to you." On the surface this looks like the parent is retaining control. However, the parent is also setting himself up to have to say no on numerous occasions. A parent in this situation better be very sure of his or her ability to say no. More than likely that parent will be saying yes repeatedly and the child will end up with more than if he/she had an allowance. In addition, there is no opportunity for the child to learn the skill of budgeting. If the parent is a soft touch, and believe me the child will find out very quickly, there are no parameters to the spending habits. Unfortunately, spending habits are developed young and the child may never learn to manage money.

The whole idea of allowance for services rendered is highly debatable. I know a single mom who agreed to an allowance for her two boys as long as one vacuumed the basement and the other cut the lawn. Some would argue that they should have done these tasks regardless of the allowance—that they should have been part of the household chores that the whole family helped with. It is difficult to know whether these young boys would recognize the importance of helping others just because it is the right thing to do. The concept of helping others ought to be an extension of the values taught to them by their parents in a variety of ways during their childhood. However, for this mother, at this particular time in their lives, allowances for services rendered brought peace and responsibility and she was able to keep control in her home.

Setting up parameters for the use of the allowance can also be helpful long-term. Putting a percentage of the money in a savings account or investment certificate increases the chances of a child developing healthy savings habits. Failure to do this leaves the child vulnerable to every type of advertising. It means that if they have more money to spend they will be in need of even larger amounts that will inevitably come from your pockets.

When your children are going out with friends, check to see what they are going to be doing. Ask them if they have any money with them, or make it clear that they can't take money with them unless you give approval. This way you can help them to consider the pros and cons of their trip prior to leaving home. Do not allow your child to leave home with large sums of money. Not only are they vulnerable to nonsensical advertising but also to individuals with very little money. They become victims to other kids who have no qualms about taxing your son or daughter for their money, and if they are at the same school as your child they may be taxing on a regular basis. Pretty soon your child won't be too interested in going to school. You would be amazed at the amount of money some teenagers bring into school each day!

When I was young, allowance was restricted to five cents or even a dime if I was lucky. It was hard to get that out of my dad, so I usually waited until one of his friends was over and he had had a couple of beers. Then I would make the request and his friend would convince him to give me the dime. Today it is quite easy to be taking out $5.00 to $20.00 bills. My kids go through these like water. I only wish I had had more influence on them with regards to saving their money. I find they are always working and occasionally asking for money yet they never have any saved. They have an insatiable desire to go out with friends even though the funds aren't there. It is only logical for them that Mom and Dad will come to the rescue!

The New School Year: An Opportunity

The start of the school year is an expensive time of year for parents. At the same time it provides an opportunity to teach our children the value of money and that there is a limited supply. Unfortunately, besides some slight grumbling, we give into this annual ritual without taking too much notice as to what happens with our initial investment. If our kids think that the school supply source is never ending then there is no need to really worry about lost items. They will always be replaced by Mom or Dad. It is important to emphasize that these supplies are special and they are lucky to have such nice things for school.

School supplies are getting more and more expensive each year and now advertisers are making bold attempts to convince us and our kids that they need more than pencils, erasers, and notebooks. I was recently looking at a back-to-school advertisement that included Walkmans, televisions, cameras, portable DVD players, computers, MP3 players and home theatre systems. The annual ritual is being used to include items totally unnecessary for school. In fact, the majority of these items would only provide a distraction from school. Our children are exposed to this type of advertising from newspapers, the Internet, and television all the time. It is important that as long as you are paying the bills you do not get sucked into this black hole of unnecessary products. It is even more important that you teach your children to avoid it as well.

Make these things special by working on the list with your child. They will then have ownership over the things that you agree to buy. The whole exerience becomes much more of a process that requires making choices, which is the most important thing to be doing. Remember, your child can't have everything he or she wants because it isn't necessary and you can't afford it. It is not something to be argued about or debated. It is simply fact. The whole experience, however, should remain positive and fun. You don't want your child feeling guilty because he/she needs legitimate school supplies. He/she will eventually come out of the process knowing; that he/she has chosen his/her supplies, that they are important to success, they are valuable, and that they should be looked after at all times.

Having worked in a suburban high school for years, I can tell you that one of the events that caretakers wait for each year is the cleaning out of the lockers. The things that get thrown out each year are incredible. Paper, pens, and notebooks are seldom recycled. The kids throw most of these things out. There are always some kids who don't bother to clean out their locker after being given several opportunities. School closes and the lockers have to be opened and cleaned out. Everything and anything is found in those lockers. Walkmans, expensive clothing, running shoes, and dictionaries are found, and the list continues endlessly. These items are recycled or given to places like the Salvation Army.

The school supply issue at first glance doesn't appear to be a major item. However it is a key part of your child's life for years and years. It is a perfect opportunity to make a point of teaching our children the value of money. At the same time, our children can be taught to recognize the difference between what they want for school and what they actually need. If the school or teacher provides a supply list, sit down with your child and go through it item by item. Review what is already available in your own home. Finally, most importantly, they have to know that what you have purchased is theirs and they need to take care of these items. Including them in the process and having them make informed decisions about their school supply list for the year makes their ownership real.

After School Fun can be a Nightmare!
Sports and extra curricular activities a child pursues outside of school can take up a tremendous amount of family time and money. It is important to remember that there is no

substitute for valuable family time together. If you are re-placing family time with all kinds of planned activities for your child then it will be more difficult to share some of those positive family values that I discussed earlier. As the kids grow up, they spend more time with friends, and so it is increasingly difficult to have any time when they are teenagers. Enjoy family time when they are younger and you will have more of an influence when they are older. Why do we want to put our kids in all these activities that might include piano lessons, drama, dance, soccer and a whole variety of other sports and activities? We want to give them the opportunity to find the things that interest them, or where they have talent. For many of us, particularly parents in the baby boomer group, we want to give our children the opportunities that we did not have. We overwhelm our children with activities of all kinds until they have no actual playtime left. Weekends with Mom and Dad have now been replaced by weekends with the coach, tutor, or music teacher!

One of the best things you can do with your child is to discuss some of the things that are possible for them to do. After that, they can make choices about what they might like to try. This shouldn't be about being able to do everything that is available in and around your neighbourhood. I remember signing my son up for hockey and I volunteered as a coach as well. It became painfully obvious that I was the only one enjoying myself out on the ice. He simply was going through the motions and even that was a struggle. Later he decided to play baseball and he was quite comfortable playing that for a number of years. Some parents had their kids in both soccer and baseball and it just didn't work. Usually there was a conflict in the schedule and the child had to miss one sport or the other. They weren't learning anything about commitment because they were letting a team down when they couldn't be there.

Let's not forget about the cost of these activities. Parents have to be prepared to shell out large sums of money for some activities. There is nothing wrong with explaining the financial limitations to your child in order to help him make the appropriate choice. This may sound trivial but I know a couple that put so much money into their child's dance lessons that they were getting into serious debt. They were paying for her to go on long-distance trips with her troupe. The couple had never had a vacation together. After quitting school and taking a summer job, she called her father two days before she was about to go on a trip to the west coast to dance. She demanded six hundred dollars immediately. The father finally came to his senses and said no, but the lesson was too little, too late. The girl told her boss she was sick and left with an advance on her salary. Her boss found out and she was fired. The girl no longer talks to her father. So much for all those years of giving.

Choosing an activity that the child can master that doesn't break the family budget is the most appropriate way to go. My daughter loved ballet from an early age. It was a natural choice for her and the cost was reasonable. Her mother and I loved to go and watch her dance, so it was really a healthy situation for the whole family. She danced well into her mid-teens and then switched over to drama. This was what made her happy and she was very good at it. We all have fond memories of her involvement in these activities. We weren't exhausted or broke because of the sheer number of activities. We were able to celebrate the skills she was learning and the fun she was having. Often that translated into more fun for the whole family because we were able to go and watch some of the shows that they presented to the public.

Key Points

To recap, here are some of the things that will help you to hang on to your hard- earned dollars. At the same time these things will help your child become an independent young adult who has the necessary skills to manage his or her own money without constantly bothering Mom and Dad for theirs.

- Parents have the most influence over their young children.
- Encourage saving by taking a portion of cash received and depositing it in a bank account.
- Have your children make choices so that they realize there are limits on what they can have.
- Give your children an allowance, but establish an understanding about the parameters of why they get an allowance and how it should be used.
- Use school supply time as an opportunity to teach restraint and budgeting skills.
- Keep the family budget in line by not going into financial ruin to pay for a child's talent or involvement in a special activity.
- Share the concept of expenses related to renting an apartment or owning a home so children have an awareness of that reality.
- Point out examples of blatant commercialism, so that your children recognize the difference between what they need and what they would actually like to have.
- Be a good role model for your children: Check

your spending: demonstrate an ability to save and spend time with your children.

- Be prepared to just say no!

4. How About the Dependent Adult Child?

If you have a dependent child who is now an adult the chances are that some of the things mentioned earlier went off the rails at a very young age. I'm discussing this now to serve as a contrast to some of the preventive ideas already discussed. The dependent adult child is a direct result of not being able to follow through with the previous suggestions when the opportunities presented themselves. The dependent adult child can be a living nightmare for parents wishing to enjoy their retirement years after raising their children. This is a child that is past the age of thirty but is still continuously dipping into your income, savings, or retirement fund. If this sounds too familiar you will probably need professional help if you don't take action soon. Remember, this is a child who could be functioning independently— if not for the financial assistance that you continue to provide. As a result, this adult child is handicapped by the lifestyle that he/she has become accustomed to.

If you are living this nightmare, then you have to ask yourself how comfortable you are with this situation. If you are not living this nightmare, and don't want to, then you should read the following anyway. At the very least, if you have young children, it should serve as motivation to follow through on some of the ideas already discussed. Parents who are burdened with the dependent adult child have not managed to find the tools to break the cycle of dependency. It sometimes gets to the point that the sound of the doorbell or phone ringing raises their anxiety level—fearing that another handout will be requested. The dependency has no boundaries as to economic status. The stories I am going to relate are just as likely to come from a family with limited financial means as they are from a wealthy family. The commonality is that the adult child knows no limits. They may feel quite comfortable taking your hard-earned savings if they are aware that they exist.

How Do I Recognize the Dependent Adult Child?

The dependent adult child sneaks up on you over time. He/she may have been someone who constantly asked for money throughout their twenties. He/she could have taken an extremely long time to finish school or he/she may not have finished school at all. This was not because he/she wasn't capable, but he /she just wasn't overly interested. He/she may have had other interests besides school, and since you were paying, there was no need to rush. Working for a living was something these people weren't too crazy about but if push came to shove, there may have been a part-time job for a little while. You seem to constantly be compensating the adult child for the things that they want to do but can't afford. There are always big ideas that might work as long as you are willing to pay for them; and a good line with no follow-through. You are disappointed because they had so much potential that has never been realized. When they were younger you may have blamed others for their lack of performance but as they get older you have become concerned that they may be the reason for their own lack of success.

The adult child is self-absorbed, wanting to fill the needs in their world as long as the parents contribute financially. Then again, they may not want to meet the responsibilities in their own world but are still willing to take funding from parents. They may not pay too much attention to bills that accumulate. They would like nothing better than for you to co-sign for a loan which more than likely they will default on, and you will end up making the payments.

It is quite possible that the adult child has their own family and that you are either paying a lot of the family bills or you are actually doing much of the parenting if you have grandchildren. This responsibility has become burdensome as you age and your financial limitations are tested.

So you have an adult child still living in your home! I bet he or she is not too anxious to leave. They may live off of you and enjoy the comforts you provide. Chances are he or she does very little around the house. He or she is a comfort to you but the dependence on you has not allowed them to move on with their life. I first read about this phenomenon occurring in Italy, where many Italian boys were staying home with their mothers until they were into their forties. They are just too comfortable at home and feel no need to become more independent.

You may be a parent who has accumulated a fair amount of wealth over the years. You love your children but none of them has really measured up to your expectations although they are doing okay. They are quite happy to be around you, particularly when you are paying. As their families grow, so do your bills for their kids' private schools. Family vacations are great as long as you pay for the whole thing. There is no privacy at the cottage because they are always there. Every once in a while it crosses your mind that they are more interested in the amount of their inheritance than they are in you!

Then there is the dependent adult child who is constantly going through money. They say they're working all kinds of jobs yet bills seem to keep piling up. You've been there before to help out, but they never seem to get out of the mess. You're beginning to wonder if there isn't something else eating up their funds. Is there an addiction problem? Is it something the family has whispered about quietly over the years, but it was never dealt with openly?

The profiles above represent a cross-section of the dependent adult children that many parents are dealing with on a daily basis. It may be that the parents wanted to provide their child with everything they could possibly afford. It could be that the parents wanted the child to remain close to home for purely selfish reasons. The only thing that remains the same is that they rarely go away easily. Later, I will look at strategies to help deal with dependent adult children who refuse to break away from the dependent relationship they have with their parents.

These Things Do Actually Happen!

The really sad thing about the dependent adult child is that they are still dependent when their parents are becoming needier. For parents, limited pension income restricts their quality of life. Health issues require more attention as parents age. The result is that they often need more support from their children—not the other way around. The following are short real life anecdotes that may sound familiar: they are happening to many families around the world every day. It is important to recognize when the cycle exists to be able to move towards a solution.

The Squatters

Mike and Barbara were like any other children growing up in a large North American City. In 1965 their young father died suddenly on a worksite. Unlike other mothers at that time, Brenda, their mother, was forced to go to work in order to pay the family bills. She worked from nine-to-five while the children were growing up. As they grew older, the children offered little except sporadic support around the house. Later, Mike started to skip classes in high school and eventually stopped going to school entirely. Brenda's house became the local all day hangout for a constantly changing rotation of students from Mike's high school. She wasn't aware of this until the situation had gone on for far too long. He worked for a few years at various jobs, but he wasn't motivated or confident enough to keep working.

Barbara was able to finish school, enrolled in college and had formal training in design. She loved art and began to paint but she was never able to maintain a steady job and gain her independence. Barbara had some relationships with men outside the home but was never able to commit for an extended period of time.

Both Mike and Barbara continue to live with their mother more than forty years after their father died. They do not work and haven't for years. They have had little luck at lasting relationships and have felt insecure about leaving their mother. Brenda uses her miniscule pension to support three adults. She needs a larger apartment to accommodate everyone. She will be in this situation until she dies.

The Deadbeats

Carol and Dave have worked all their lives for the same company; Dave in the finance department and Carol as a secretary. Retirement has finally arrived for the two of them after years of dedication to the company. They are well-liked by all employees, and there will be a big retirement celebration.

However, there is something that most employees at the company don't know about Carol and Dave's private lives. They have a son and daughter-in-law who have not accepted their responsibilities as parents. Their two grand-daughters would have been placed in foster homes were it not for Carol and Dave's intervention along with that of their daughter in-law's parents.

As a result, these two children have been taken in by the four grandparents so that they would stay with their families. Carol and Dave's recent years have meant going to interviews at elementary schools and paying for all the needs of their granddaughters. They take their grand-daughters to Disney World when they might otherwise be enjoying a restful holiday away together.

Retirement for them means a continuation of looking after their ten-year-old granddaughters with many years of care still to come. Their son and daughter-in-law continue to live a life on the edge of society with little involvement in the lives of their children. Carol and Dave have to negotiate visitation with the other set of grandparents so that they are able to see their two granddaughters together. It's not a retire-ment they would have dreamed about ten years ago, but it has become their reality.

The Sponge

If you are a sponge you generally have to squeeze pretty hard to get what you want. Robert's situation is no exception. He is divorced from his wife and she is unable to have custody of their son. In fact, she is not allowed to have time alone with her son. Robert is unemployed himself and has had to move in with his parents.

Joyce and Al have been trying to cover for Robert all his life. They are frustrated and embarrassed by their son's inability to live up to his responsibilities. Al worked all his life in a factory and has been retired for some years. Life has not been easy for him. Al recently finished a long year of cancer treatments and is struggling to regain his strength.

Al and Joyce have had to move away from the small town they retired to a few years go to move to a large city where they have no sense of community. They are worried about their son losing custody of their grandson and are moving so they can provide a home address for their son to help him maintain custody of his son. Once they arrive in the city from their uprooting they face parenting duties all over again. They are responsible for making sure their grandson gets registered in school. When Robert is told about school fees, he sends his parents instead, failing to mention payment is needed. Embarrassed, they leave and return with the money—knowing that they have entered a land of no return. Retirement is slowly taking their love of life away. A sponge will do that to you in so many ways.

The Addict

The addict is difficult to nail down because he or she is always in denial. Sandra and Ben are getting more nervous when their daughter calls because she always needs more money. Their daughter is 55 years old and Sandra and Ben are in their eighties. They can't understand why she can't get her finances in order. Sandra and Ben have a limited pension and can't keep dishing out.

Their daughter, Martine, seems to be working all the time. However, the more she works the more bills she appears to accumulate. They used to enjoy her company when she came over for dinner, but now the demands are increasing. At first she would ask for twenty to forty dollars but now the demands have moved into the hundreds of dollars per visit.

Recently a bill collector showed up at their door. Ben had co-signed a loan for Martine but she had not made the payments in three months. Sandra and Ben are growing increasingly concerned about Martine's behaviour. They are now in disagreement as to whether to give Martine more money.

Martine is a gambler who has tried to get help. Ben and Sandra sometimes pay for things that Martine needs. They are reluctant to give her money at this point because Martine is likely to give in to her addiction. The cycle of giving is endless because no amount of money can satisfy the addiction. Ben and Sandra don't understand what an addiction is; and they really miss their daughter. They talk about her as if she is a ghost from the past because they have very little positive to say about her present situation. It makes them extremely sad to see what their daughter has done with her life.

The Opportunist

The opportunist comes out when the payoff is large enough. For instance, Isabelle is turning eighty. Her family has not even discussed what to do for her birthday and probably wouldn't even have gotten together. However, Isabelle has announced that she will celebrate her birthday in the Bahamas. She will pay for anyone to go and celebrate with her. All of a sudden, everyone is excited about the birthday.

Even the son-in-laws are coming to celebrate. Isabelle will drop about thirty thousand dollars to see her family celebrate with her. Each of her children, who are now in their fifties, is quite capable of paying their own way, but they would never bother to get together if they had to do that. However, there is the possibility of a large inheritance in the not too distant future.

In a similar situation, Gordon is a self-made millionaire. He used to bring his family to holiday on the east coast when his four children were younger before becoming a millionaire. A few years ago one of his sons suggested they all go down to the ocean together for a holiday in the summer. Everyone agreed they wanted to go. The only catch was that Gordon was going to pay for everyone's oceanfront cottage. Of course, there was also the small matter of accommodating the dozen grandchildren.

The Freeloader

Susan got into the habit of hitting her father up for money when she was a teenager. By the time she married, he had helped finance a long-term stay in Europe as well as a home on the west coast. Susan's father died about ten years ago but her mother is still alive. At ninety, her mother's wealth has dwindled to a modest home and a run-down country property that was her husband's favourite retreat.

Susan's mother was about to sell the property six years ago to raise money for her dwindling savings because Susan and her husband had used up a lot of her father's retirement savings. Susan arrived from five hundred miles away with her two children and husband and they've been living in the house rent free for the last six years. They moved back to the city in order to secure work but not before getting the deed to the property changed to their name. Let's hope Susan's mother has enough funds to pay the taxes on her small home!

The Dreamer

Peter has big ideas, but he doesn't have the financial resources to put his plans into place. In addition to that he has had very little formal education beyond high school. He talks a good line and is very well read, but his understanding of sound business practice is shaky. He spends much of his time conjuring up schemes that will help him become financially independent. Now in his mid-forties, he has seldom had success in the business world.

Unfortunately, his parents, Brian and Cathy, are the ones that are asked to make financial contributions to his projects. His favourite expression is, "I just need…" The sad thing is that his needs seem to be constantly growing. Brian and Cathy live on two teacher's pensions, and although they have been very good about saving, their money is dwindling at an alarming rate. Eighty percent of their savings have been used up by Peter. They claim they are not worried, but at seventy Cathy is beginning to have trouble sleeping at night. They have always believed that they should support their children but now feel that the support has gone too far.

The Picker

The picker is common in many families. Lena goes into her parent's home and browses as if on a shopping spree. The only difference is that the picker has no intention of buying anything. The picker is constantly picking through your things trying to convince you that it would really be better if you gave them certain things now. Let's put it this way, your house is always a little less cluttered after they leave!

Lena is only interested in certain items of course. She particularly likes fine jewellery, art and furniture. By the way, if her parents don't want to give the item to her right away, she is quite happy to write her name on the back of the item for future consideration. She is also eager to claim things for her own children. Inviting this child over for dinner can be extremely costly. Pickers enjoy coming over when their siblings aren't around, so they can pick in leisure. Slowly but surely, the finer things from your home begin to be transported to your son or daughter's home. The other kids are often wondering where things have disappeared, until they are invited into the picker's home.

The Neverlander

This child just refused to grow up. If John could find Peter Pan, he would be off to Neverland in a flash despite the fact he is in his sixties. John has had mixed success with maintaining a job. He is very hard to dislike because he is so likeable. He seems to have a lot of friends and is accepted in a variety of circles.

The problem is that a lot of John's playing costs money and he never has enough to go around. That's where Bert and Elaine come in. They end up financing a lot of the fun things that the neverlander is doing. They will continue to do this as long as they are willing and able.

I've known parents who have given their child a monthly allowance because all he wants to do at fifty-five is play. Other parents finance trips or special events as they come along. Sometimes the neverlander is able to repay and other times not. Unfortunately, the neverlander becomes more difficult to deal with as employment becomes tougher and funds dwindle.

Summary

These are examples of the realities that older parents sometimes endure to remain close to their children. Over the years the relationship evolved from a truly loving relationship to one where a series of transactions were exchanged to maintain contact. The invitation for dinner was based on an understanding that there would be something in it for the son or daughter. It was no longer there just for the sake of spending time together.

The dependent adult child can absolutely care about their parents. However the important thing to remember is that very often these adult children are extremely self-absorbed. They do not consider the fact that their parents may be financially strapped. They couldn't imagine that their parents would like to retire to peace, enjoy their grandchildren at special times, and not be burdened for the rest of their years with more mouths to feed. Some parents help finance a child's business and they meet with financial independence. Unfortunately a large number of stories are not as positive, and the burden can be crippling. Later, I will look at strategies to try and avoid falling into a situation where you are the one who is constantly giving while your children are the ones doing all the taking.

Key Points

- Dependency in an adult child can handicap them for life.
- Dependent adult children can seriously affect your

quality of life as well as your bank account.

• Sometimes the adult child knows no limits in trying to access a parent's hard-earned income or pension.

• Look for the traits of the dependent adult child in the behaviour of teenagers and young adults.

• Dependent adult children can come in various forms. All of them need to be dealt with to stop the dependency.

5. Teenagers

Teenagers come in all shapes and sizes but they basically want to fit in with their friends. This is important because their friends exert a large influence on them. This is where the generation gap begins. It really is about parents and teenagers not being able to communicate what their needs or values are to each other. We may have had the sweetest kids when they were in elementary school but once they hit high school all hell can break loose!

Working with teenagers for so long has made me realize that a lot of their self-esteem today is actually connected to the appearance of financial independence. There is a tremendous amount of pressure on them to have the toys and fashions that are marketed to teenagers in magazines, the Internet, and on television. Let's face it, when a television show becomes popular with teenagers it really isn't about a teenager living with the bare minimum. There's a reason that shows with fancy lifestyles are popular with teenagers— it is the lifestyle they want to live.

This age group has more cash to spend on toys than most others. Their financial responsibilities are limited by what they want to buy each week. Their income is restricted by what their parents are willing to give them or by what they are making at a part-time job. This combination of circumstances has completely duped them into believing they can afford an outlandish lifestyle.

Unfortunately, it often becomes difficult to deal with teenagers who have bought into the affluent lifestyle. The line between their needs and their wants no longer exists. They may ask for your opinion on something but what they really want is for you to give them the answer they want to hear. The result of giving the wrong answer can result in a major outburst or battle.

Teenagers tend to see things in black or white. They can either go to the mall or they can't go to the mall. They don't really want to hear that you'd like the family to have dinner or watch a movie together if they have other plans. The fact that you may not have money to give them is totally unacceptable. They just don't get it! Whatever happened to the bank machine?

Teenagers can differ in terms of what their needs are. A computer nerd has different needs than the skater punk. Although both have a need for friends, their friends can have extremely different interests. We can sometimes, but not always, see this in the way they dress: skaters generally wear gear that identifies them with the skater crowd. They have an outfit that says, "I don't have to follow the rules!"

Computer nerds need to know what the latest technology is to upgrade their PCs. Going out on a Friday night may only interfere with the computer programming that they are doing. Skater kids would probably not think of staying home on Friday night unless it was with the gang. The computer nerd is content to spend more time alone with less need for friends.

The other thing that is important to remember is that teenagers can morph into any image they feel is appealing. For instance, when my son was about fourteen he was into the whole rapper image. Once he had gone as far as he felt comfortable with that look, he changed to a more progressive rock image. All this, of course, takes place so that teenagers can find their own comfort zone.

It is important that they experiment with how they look so that they develop their own identity or style which may happen to be closely related to a particular movie or rock star's look, but it enables them to evolve into the person they will become as an adult. The changes can be frustrating and expensive for the parent if the process is ongoing and the teenager is never satisfied.

Teenagers want to be independent until things don't quite work out. At that point they are quick to call in Mom and Dad to bail them out. And this is a time when you need to be there for them. Knowing where your teenager is and who he/she is hanging out with is really essential in this day and age. An involved parent is really helping to make sure that his/her son or daughter is making the right choices as they begin to spend more time out of the family home.

One of the things that I have discovered is that what we think will make a teenager happy is not at all what they would really like. Teenagers today have had a much greater influence from outside sources than we are aware of. Having a very comfortable home with their own bedroom and play-room isn't necessarily enough for teenagers today. Home today, for teenagers, represents a separation from their friends. So although they may be at home, they quickly move to technologies such as computers and cell phones to get back in touch with the friends whom they have just left at school. The result can be hours locked away in the privacy of their own room communicating with their friends all night long. Not only is there little room for homework, but there is also very little time for family.

The alienation within your home can be so dramatic that the idea of family as you once knew it has become a foreign concept within the walls of your home. Constant reminders and arguments are endured to achieve a semblance of cooperation. Even the simplest of tasks becomes frustrating. It is not rare as a parent to have the feeling that your teenager is a stranger who has moved into the family. You sometimes wish for your teenager to be out so that you are able to have some peace. Then, when he or she is not there, you can't stop worrying! Unfortunately, time away from home can only increase the alienation.

Cell Phone

The need to stay in contact with peers or anyone else, regardless of the crowd you are hanging with defines this age group. I recently heard one teenager berating his mother because he wanted to talk to her and her cell phone was off. She tried to explain to him that she had gone for a quiet walk and didn't want to be disturbed by the cell phone. He earnestly explained that you should never turn your cell phone off or go anywhere without it.

Teenagers don't really have a lot to say to one another except to maintain contact and pick up the latest gossip. They obviously use it to plan outings to the mall. I believe there is a fair amount of status that goes along with the number of people that you are able to contact on your cell phone because teens always seem to be talking to people who they never see socially. I'll talk more about dealing with cell phone issues later in this book.

The Internet

I couldn't possibly imagine the variety of things that a

teenager has access to on the Internet. The possibilities are endless and some teenagers are addicted to spending all of their time at the computer. They leave themselves and your home open to all kinds of unseen predators on a daily basis. Chat lines are the favourite of many teenagers, and the more mature ones restrict their chats to friends who they are familiar with. Others, particularly those with few close friends, find chat rooms with strangers.

Recently, a group of teenagers at a private high school in my city built up a large debt on a poker site. The teenagers had been playing regularly and got carried away. On line gambling has become much more popular in recent years and teenagers are not immune to its temptation. Teenagers susceptible to this temptation might have their own credit card and spend long hours at the computer.

The "A" Student

The student who is getting straight A's is not immune to any of the changes, temptations or expenses that other teenagers go through. Their parents are just fortunate to have a child who is focussed when it comes to school. Really, their financial needs may surpass other teenagers' because they may be involved in so many school activities. Today, many high schools offer programs that cost a fair amount of money to participate in. Band and elite sports programs in most schools come with a high cost. As mentioned earlier, my son's school band went to England for a music competition while my daughter's went to New York. Their mother and I were fortunate in that they contributed toward these trips with money earned through part-time jobs.

Extra-Curricular Activities

Most teenagers need to be involved with something structured in their spare time. The difficulty lies in managing the expensive activities as they get older. Without a doubt it is extremely important to attempt to keep your teenager involved in a structured activity but as the activities get more sophisticated the cost of the activity can increase dramatically. Helping your teenager make appropriate choices for their skill level as well as within financial constraints is necessary.

For teenagers who have grown up in organized activities it can be a shock when the funds are no longer available or their skill level is not accomplished enough to participate. The girl who has believed she would become a prima ballerina or the football quarterback who can no longer compete have time as well as self-esteem issues to deal with. It is important as a parent to help re-focus the energy and re-establish the self-esteem through some other endeavour that your teenager undertakes. It is always important to reinforce the fact to your teenager that he or she is special as a person and not because they dance or play sports.

The Fashion Influence

As I indicated earlier, every teenager wants to create their own identity. Fashion is the number one way to convey who they are. Fashion variety is endless today—and very expensive. I was talking to one seventeen-year-old who feels he must wear Versace and Hugo Boss clothes. I have no idea how he came to this conclusion, but he feels quite good about it.

The problem with this need to wear only extremely high end clothing is that it really is not the reality in which most teenagers live. The teenager mentioned above didn't even have a part-time job. His parents were supportive and he is able to use birthday money to buy these items. I'm not sure what they did when they went shopping with him. The reality is that these are two middle class people with very little extra income to waste on designer clothes.

The Part-Time Job

Without a doubt teenagers today are more connected to our economy than ever before. I don't know what would happen to small business owners if they were not able to hire teenagers to staff their business. If you don't believe me, just go to the mall on any given day and look at the teenagers running the various stores. It is sometimes difficult to find an adult in the mall. A recent study in the United States found that at least 56% of high school senior students had part-time jobs.

The part-time job takes teenagers away from their home for long periods of time and the money they earn allows them the freedom to pursue other interests outside the home—further separating them from their parents. They feel so empowered by their financial independence that they often get caught up believing they can afford to do anything. Pretty soon they're talking about buying audio-video components for their rooms. New clothes and DVDs are a constant addition to your home. They may even ask for an advance on their salary in order to purchase something.

The part-time job is like a house of cards. The foundation can be pulled out from under them at any time. Teenagers rarely think of that happening as they dream about their fantasy lifestyle. They ignore the warnings about arriving late to work or not wearing the correct uniform. By this time they have a lifestyle of needing money for toys and activities and if they lose their jobs, Mom and Dad are expected to pick up the pieces.

Driving

Learning to drive has always been a huge milestone in any teenager's life. Along with the danger of being on the road at all hours comes the financial responsibility of operating a vehicle. The price of gasoline alone restricts movement. Insurance can run into the thousands of dollars for teenage boys. The financial obligation is tremendous even if they don't own their own car.

Driving allows your teenager to wander further away from home. The teenager in need of acceptance will suddenly find he or she has many more friends, anxious to be driven everywhere. Mom and Dad are freed up on Friday night when they might otherwise be a taxi service, but there is no peace of mind.

Unknown Influences

The Internet is not the only place where teenagers can be influenced by unknown sources. Each day they go to school with hundreds of teenagers from a variety of backgrounds. If your son or daughter is looking for something, then school is probably the place where they are going to find it. It takes a strong teenager to say no when faced with some of the temptations peers thrust in front of them.

Sexual promiscuity, drugs, criminal activity, alcohol and cigarettes are all there for the taking for those interested in going down that road. The good thing is that most teenagers don't venture too far into this, but there are always some attracted to this lifestyle. Along with the financial burden, there is a high emotional cost for the whole family when these habits get out of control. The weight can be all-encompassing and any attempts to thwart the behaviour can be met with obstacles.

Summary
The real-life challenges for the parents of teenagers is a far cry from the fantasy lifestyle many of their sons and daughters dream about. This can be a period of tremendous hope and happiness—as well as a time of disappointment and sadness. Often our emotional roller-coaster is directly connected to their success and failure. In the meantime, teenagers are generally oblivious to our feelings and continue along the same path that they have decided to follow.

Besides the important financial obligation, it is so important to maintain the lines of communication between yourself and your teenager. Without a doubt, it is always better to know where your son or daughter is. Their friends are really your guide to the type of activities your teenager is involved in. If you seriously suspect that your son's friends are involved in drugs, then chances are so is he!

The need to be accepted, have cool or unique looks, belong to a certain crowd, or have the toys that teenagers identify with all come with a price tag. Parents can end up paying the price for a lifestyle their teenager believes he or she should be living. Making sure your teenager understands the parameters of house rules is absolutely necessary. Failure to do this only leads to ambiguity and the rules cease to exist.

Once rules have disappeared, teenagers have more license to be out of the house more often. Being out of the house provides teenagers with the opportunity to come under the influence of people you would otherwise hope they would avoid. This can lead to all kinds of bad habits that will haunt your home and could affect their lives for years. The financial and emotional fallout can be tremendous.

I'll talk about strategies in the chapters ahead that will help deal with teenagers to not break the family bank. Careful planning and frank discussions are needed to put the brakes on a consumer frenzy that, at times, appears to have no limits. Regardless, confronting a teenager on life-style choices can be emotionally draining for parents.

Key Points

- For many teenagers, because of intense commercialization, self-esteem can be directly connected to their discretionary income.
- The fantasy lifestyle teenagers crave is a direct result of the movies, television and other videos they see daily.
- Teenagers go through many different phases that will probably change depending on their influences and who they are hanging with at any given time.
- Teenagers are actually looking for themselves by experimenting with different crazes, friends and activities.
- Parents are replaced by friends as the most influential people in their lives.
- Teenagers stay connected to friends through cell phones and the Internet when not in school.
- Part-time jobs can often give a teenager a false sense of security in terms of what they are able to

afford. The result is that they can over-spend.

• Teenagers who excel can also prove costly because of the expense of the extra-curricular programs they enrol in.

• Delay driving lessons as much as possible if you want to keep expenses down.

• Keep a close eye on your teenager's lifestyle as unknown influences can creep in quickly.

6. The Young Adult

The young adult feels the world is his or her oyster. They are only limited by their own imagination. Whether working in a menial job, training in a trade school or going to university the young adult is generally optimistic about his or her future. They are often not content with the creature comforts that we have acquired. The home and garden in the suburbs with the mini-van is not their idea of the good life. They are looking for a lifestyle that reflects the influences they've had through their teenage years. The young adult is from twenty to thirty, and usually feels ready to experience whatever life has to offer.

Their world consists of some combination of school and work. They might still be living at home and thinking about getting their own place, or they may have already moved out. Those who are still living at home might have a fair amount of discretionary income. Others who've moved out are either doing extremely well or struggling from paycheque to paycheque, but there is very little that can slow down a lifestyle which includes a hefty entertainment budget. This budget may include both home and public entertainment. This age group still wants to be at the trendiest spots with their friends whenever they get together.

This generation really does want to do it all. One of the differences from other generations is that they want to do it all now! They are not like the sixties generation that would hitchhike around Europe or North America. Youth hostels were the destination of choice to save money. This generation wants to go to expensive resorts and live well. Parents of young adults know that they have to hold onto their wallets to limit the handouts.

The American Idol

This is also the generation that believes anything is possible if you will it to happen. Fifty years ago Elvis had to find Sam Phillips at Sun Records to get recorded. Today most young adults know someone with the technology to record; it may be it in their basement or garage, but it is available. They have what I call The American Idol Syndrome—many of them truly believe they could be a superstar. Previous generations dreamed about this but these young adults believe it is possible.

A testament to this is the sheer number of young adults who flock to these talent shows believing they have a serious chance of winning. It amazes me when I hear the stories of the distances people travel to participate in such events. The sad thing is that many of these individuals have very little talent. And even worse, Mom and Dad are right there encouraging the fantasy with their wallets and blind praise. It's at this time as young adults, that as parents, you had better hope that your child is becoming more realistic about his or her future.

It doesn't help that some of the pop stars they grew up on had a very little talent. For a while there, it was like every twenty-year-old white guy in the suburbs wanted to be a rap star. Many of these young adults were trying to be like Eminem. It never occurred to them that he must have a rare talent to rise from the conditions he lived in and make it in a predominantly black music genre.

Fantasy Sports Nuts

What better way to be in denial about your own athletic abilities than by participating in any type of fantasy sport that you can imagine. Of course this is the generation that has grown up on Playstation. Their eye-hand coordination has made them masters of any sport they want to master. There are no limits to the number of hours they are prepared to give to sitting in front of a screen with a controller in their hand. They haven't clued in to the fact that it is precisely this obsession with playing fantasy sports games that has prevented many of them from excelling in any real sports activities.

Fantasy football in North America has become a huge phenomenon with this age group, as has on-line poker. Both rely on chance as much, if not more, than skill. Both are about the possibility of being the champion, rather than on the actual competition. They have a component of gambling that is disturbing. Now that the media has taken hold and added star power and money to make it more alluring for a greater audience young adults have bought it hook, line, and sinker!

The disturbing thing for this group and their parents is that the similarities with uncontrolled gambling are so close that it creates a disturbing precedent. Is the rapid rise of casinos in North America specifically to tap into these baby boomer offspring? If so, parents will be under tremendous pressure to help their children because once an addiction occurs the temptation is around just about every corner.

The Happy Wanderers

Holidays are not foreign to the young adult. They are the first generation to really make use of the Internet to plan

their trips. They have access to such a wide variety of destinations and book holidays regardless of whether they are in
school, working, or have part-time jobs. They seem to be
able to adjust schedules to their boss's satisfaction, take a
holiday someplace exotic, and still retain their jobs.

It is not too surprising to see young people travelling
several times a year while going to school and holding down
part-time jobs. Don't forget, Mom and Dad are probably
paying their tuition, food, and clothes, and they might be
living at home rent free. If the money is not going on toys,
it must be going on travel. So parents pay regardless of
whether or not the young adult has paid for the trip.

Mr. & Ms. Independent

Mr. and Ms Independent think they can make it on their
own. Why should they give their parents rent when they
can have their freedom? They want to enjoy having their
own apartment. That logic usually ends up costing Mom
and Dad more in the long run because the young adult has
not factored in all the costs of living alone. Telephone, cable,
heating and electricity costs all add up. Add the cost of
moving, and furnishing and renting an apartment—a
young adult can be waist deep in debt in no time at all.

I've been on the Costco and Wal-Mart trail for household goods with my kids as they prepare to face the world of
independence. It's a tough one for everyone involved. First,
you have to live with the idea that your child is leaving
home even though you think the timing is not right. Then,
to maintain peace, you have to show support by helping
him or her with the things that they are going to need on a
daily basis. You find yourself shopping for microwaves and
going to garage sales to look for the articles of comfort that

they will inevitably end up needing.

The other important piece of the puzzle young people seldom consider is the difficulty of living alone. Usually they only consider the excitement and romantic vision of having their own place. It can be a daunting task to keep everything afloat and take care of yourself for the first time in your life. Video games just don't seem the same without Mom or Dad in the kitchen making dinner.

The Perennial Student

Some of these young adults have it so good that there isn't any rush to finish school. When I was in grade seven a teacher explained to the class that it costs quite a bit every year you stay in school. I tuned into that lesson immediately. He explained that every year you stay in school needlessly, you delay entering the workforce, which decreases your total income over a lifetime. I had never heard anything like this before in my life. I never forgot it and was determined not to delay my stay in school unnecessarily.

Recently, I heard about a student I had taught about twenty years ago. He was still in school and Mom and Dad had been financing his education since high school. Twenty years is amazing enough, but for parents to finance such a journey is quite remarkable. Even scarier was the fact that his schooling was not finished. I wonder what lessons have been learned over time by both the parents and the student. How does one go from such a lifestyle to a working career?

Mr. & Ms In-Between

Well, it finally happened, your son or daughter has graduated from school. The only problem is that they don't seem to be doing very much about finding employment. All that time, effort and money poured into years of education and not much is happening. This can become an endless cycle if your son or daughter cannot come up with a job. The longer it takes the more difficult it becomes. Self-confidence dwindles as the weeks pass without a job.

The crazy thing is that just when you think your financial responsibilities as a parent should be ending, a young adult in this situation may demand even more. This can cause stress, particularly if you and your spouse disagree on the level of support you should provide. I've known families that have had to endure years of frustration because a child refused to be more assertive about finding a job.

Nowhere Man

It is sad that there are young adults still living at home who have no motivation to move on with their lives. They have not pursued education following their high school years. The workforce has been met with a mixed degree of success. Their world consists of an endless cycle of all-night activities combined with a mid-afternoon wake up call.

To make matters worse, this young adult hangs out with friends with the same attitude. They can occupy your home playing video games and watching movies until all hours of the morning when things are going relatively well in their lives. Without a dramatic change of attitude this situation can deteriorate rapidly—your son or daughter can become desperate to have what he or she feels is needed or wanted. The lure of crime, gambling, drugs and alcohol become real possibilities. As an involved parent you may already be aware that this is happening.

The Miracle

You may be that lucky parent who has been able to raise a child with very little difficulty through the years. Your child has grown into a fine young man or woman who has brought little stress to the family. This child has always had focus and a degree of talent. He or she is an independent thinker who is not afraid to take challenges. This may lead in different directions that you are unfamiliar with but that you are confident can provide them with a positive experience.

The interesting thing about this child is that he or she may not have always had an easy time of it, particularly at school. However, somewhere along the way, and this could have happened at any time, they realized that they had the capability to do something with their life. Generally, this son or daughter had quite a positive disposition and a variety of interests. These interests kept them happily occupied for endless hours particularly during the vulnerable teenage years.

Not every child will require parents to make an extreme financial commitment. The miracle young adult is exactly that child. This child may be more inclined to have had steady part-time jobs throughout their schooling. They may have also saved for and bought many of the things they felt were needed without putting extra pressure on the household budget.

Once these young adults finally find employment they might be quite content to live at home for a few years and pay the rent that is requested. This young adult may have bigger plans to save and buy a condo once they have enough money for the down payment. They are always looking ahead and are not content to stay at home and live off parents for an extended period of time. They want to make their own way in life.

Summary

There is no magic pill that a parent can give a child to help him or her become an independent young adult. It is important that these young people experiment with who they are and where they want to go with their lives. This is all part of the process of growing up. For those of us with children in their twenties we are aware that the process of growing up takes much longer today than in previous generations.

There is almost an unwritten code with this generation that there is no need to rush into adulthood. They are too busy enjoying the trappings of the computer age to commit to a lifestyle that would limit their play time. Responsibilities connected to home and family are not at the top of their priority list.

In the meantime, the price tag for their lifestyle has become a burden for most parents, regardless of the type of young adult you may have raised. The difference lies in the degree of joy the financial support has provided. This depends on what the young adult eventually does with this support. It can be a frustrating time for parents eager to move on to retirement years.

This generation of young people can, single-handedly, derail some of the best laid retirement plans. Years of support in various forms means thousands of dollars. Supporting the lifestyle of a third and possibly even a fourth adult in the home can seriously deplete savings.

The average middle income parents cannot withstand the pressure and the level of support often demanded for any great length of time. A working class family would get into serious debt by giving into the demands of this generation. Middle-class parents could never afford to retire if they were unable to stop the dependency. Wealthy families would have to hope for an alternative solution to stop the financial bleeding.

Key Points

- The young adult is often looking beyond the comforts of your home and what you are able to provide to be satisfied.
- The young adult wants to still hang out with friends, while beginning to enjoy their vision of what their adult life should be.
- This generation considers themselves to be capable of anything and are believers in the American Idol syndrome.
- Young adults want an independent lifestyle before they can afford it.
- There is a disturbing amount of marketing towards this generation to get them involved in gambling; particularly through the Internet.
- Some young adults take a tremendous amount of time to move on with their life, placing increased financial stress on their parents.
- There are always young adults who have been able to keep things together without causing their parents too much financial stress.

7. Reflecting on the Profiles

It should be very sobering to reflect on the profiles I have just outlined. Our children have some traits of all the characters I have described. There are no limits to what they will use to get what they want. You may be one of the lucky parents whose child, whether a teenager or adult, functions independently without your direct financial assistance. This allows you to continue with your life plans without too much interference from your children. Planning is usually a formula for disappointment—we can't always control health setbacks, relationship difficulties, or job displacements.

Regardless of the pitfalls of planning, we do spend a fair amount of time planning home renovations, retirement, job advancement, health status and financial stability. When our children are young we dream of the very best for them. A lot of our time and energy goes toward providing them with the opportunities outlined earlier. At this point life seems to come full circle for us and our own satisfaction—barring any unforeseen difficulties.

Being Technologically Challenged
The roller-coaster ride of everyday life often doesn't allow us to catch the subtle changes or adjustments we may be having with our own children. A relative's 18-year-old daughter wanted to buy her boyfriend something for his

birthday. The daughter doesn't work so she asked her mother if she could have fifty dollars to buy her boyfriend an iPod. What the mother didn't know was that iPods don't sell for fifty dollars; she also didn't know that her daughter saw the iPod on eBAY—a live auction where the bidding hadn't stopped. Mother agreed to give her daughter her credit card so she could purchase the iPod. The end result was that the iPod cost two hundred and forty-seven dollars plus taxes and delivery.

You may ask yourself why this mother didn't anticipate such a thing happening. The reality is that it is impossible to anticipate such a flagrant disregard for your hard- earned money. When you have worked all your life to have a modest home and a half-decent job, you assume, wrongly, that your children appreciate and respect the hard work it has taken to maintain the lifestyle that the family is able to enjoy.

Our lives are caught up in a fast-paced society that expects us to be everything to everyone. To maintain balance in our lives and not be tempted by the excess that many people fall victim to, we must develop an inner braking system that says no to the needless toys we are barraged with. Usually we learn to do this over time by trial and error. If you are strong willed, you may be successful at maintaining control over your spending habits. If you are not skilled at managing your own financial affairs you are in danger of becoming something like the sponge or the opportunist described earlier.

Store Open: Twenty-Four Hours a Day

The teenage daughter described above has not absorbed the lessons that life provides to realize when things have gotten out of hand. It could be argued that she lied to her mother and she knew exactly what she was doing but, the fact remains that all the things teenagers dream about become real on their screens at the click of a mouse. Thousands of items are pushed their way every time they go to a new website. The other reality is that the daughter was given the means to access these things with her mother's permission to use the credit card. Many of us have been to an auction, and it is easy to get the adrenalin going and get caught up in the bidding as the auction progresses. It takes a skilled and experienced participant to resist the temptation and not go beyond pre-determined limits.

So why do we repeatedly allow ourselves to be on the hook for sometimes five times the initial understanding as with the teenager, her mother and the iPod? We seldom reflect on the rapidly changing society we live in and the effect it is having on everyone, particularly our children. In this situation, an initial reflection could have been: "Why is my daughter, who has absolutely no money to her name, even considering a fifty dollar gift for her boyfriend?" Once you come to the realization that there is something wrong with the picture, you can reflect further on the more serious problems of values and responsibility. When you think about it, there is something seriously lacking in even thinking that she must buy such a gift. This is further complicated by a total lack of respect for her mother's money, and putting her into more debt. Then there is the further consideration— was this an innocent mistake ignited by bad judgement, or was this total manipulation of a parent who is too naïve or busy to, at the very least, check the credibility of the story?

The iPod story is a simple one that is a reflection of much more complicated social values. It is necessary for parents to consider the world in which their children live and how it has affected who they are. Ultimately we have the most influence on our young children's lives, so we must take responsibility for the way our children live their lives. This is often difficult for us to do because we seldom want to see the things that don't quite mesh with our own value systems.

The technology that young adults and teenagers have mastered was not available to previous generations and many parents do not understand the limitless possibilities that exist for young people daily on the Internet. What is second nature for them is often unfamiliar ground for us so we must consciously consider all of the ramifications of their actions, particularly on the Internet. When they are parents they will have experienced all the painful lessons of the Internet and be able to anticipate their children's activities—though by that time technology will throw some new curves into the mix that will allow even greater and faster access to everything imaginable. Their children will continue the cycle.

By isolating incidents like the iPod purchase, parents should be able to assess their children. Look for this type of request from your own children and see if the pattern is similar. The sad thing is that it is extremely difficult to admit to the limitations of our children because as parents, we need to believe that they will rise above their dependency and eventually stand on their own two feet. But the pattern can't continue for too long or the dependency will never be eliminated—this is exactly why they repeatedly attempt to treat us like ATMs!

Recognize Your Child
The very fact that you may be able to recognize the type of

85

child you are dealing with will enable you to help that child overcome their unhealthy dependency on you. This realization will also allow you to develop some strategies that will protect you from children who persistently prey on your bank account to enhance their own lifestyle. A realistic understanding of your child will help you develop a plan that remains consistent and forces your child to look within to move on with life. A child who cannot do this needs more than your money to bring happiness. You are far better off dealing with those shortcomings when the child is young enough to make a successful change.

The most extreme example of not dealing with children who are constantly trying to make their own rules and are in denial about their own behaviour is the Menendez brothers' case. These two brothers eventually murdered their parents for their inheritance. This came after years of their manipulative father's denial about his sons' limitations. The father used his power and money to shape the boys into cold-blooded killers. They always wanted more and were taught to do whatever it took to get it. Both were infatuated with life in the fast lane that they could never hope to achieve because of their pathetic work ethic. They had no choice but to depend on their father's money, yet he was the very person they resented because he had controlled and manipulated their lives. However, their dependency had become so extreme that their greed and perverse upbringing eventually caused them to turn on the parents who had provided them with their lavish lifestyle.

Key Points
- As parents, we want the best for our children.
- For the most part, our children are more techno-

logically advanced than we are.

- Our children have access to the world through the Internet twenty-four hours a day, and that includes shopping.
- Parents need to take the time to understand what their children are doing particularly when they are on the Internet.
- Look for behaviour patterns that could signal unrealistic dependency.
- Financial dependency knows no economic boundaries—as wealthy and working class families can fall victim to it.

8. Understanding your Own Motives

For any parent to break the cycle of their children's dependency, it is important to look within yourself to understand your motives for continuing to feed the need. What baggage are we carrying that caused this dynamic to develop? Is the dependency that has developed a need that we have expressed through our parenting style? Have we given our children the message that we want them to remain dependent on us for a long period?

The dependent relationship between children and parents is a very natural dynamic when the children are young. Even more obvious is the undying love we have for our children throughout their lives. Just as natural is the need to let our children become more independent as they move into their teen and young adult years. If, as parents, we begin to lose our perspective on how to foster this transition stage it becomes difficult for our children to become independent. This unnatural dependency may have been fostered from a very young age, as I have already described.

Ultimately, if dependency continues to be nurtured at the very time when independence should be celebrated, the transition period will be compromised. The following characteristics, combined with the love we have for our children, are some of the reasons why we have difficulty letting go. At the same time these characteristics are the very reason why our children remain financially dependent for so long. To stop the cycle of our children's financial dependency it is important to examine the reasons why we may have difficulty changing our own behaviour.

Fear

Fear of letting go is common among parents. Those first parties and trips in a friend's car cause us constant worry. It is precisely these experiences that allow the teenager to take the necessary steps into adult life because during these social activities they learn to say no and pick the friends who they want to hang with. They have to make these decisions on their own—and they will probably make mistakes, but ultimately that is what will help them move forward with their lives.

Besides the fear of letting go is the fear of saying no. Depending on how we have brought up our children, it is possible that the child has the power in the relationship. Like my young friend Steven, a child will learn early which buttons to push to get what he or she wants. Once the child is a teen, it is much more difficult to say no because they've been given everything for so long. And let's not forget one other thing—these kids are a lot bigger. I've been in many interviews with parents and they have told me that they are afraid of their teenage son's temper and size.

Control

Control can show itself in many forms. A parent may control by making a comment that causes his child to fear rejection. Control may come by constantly placing demands on a teenager or young adult once they begin to move towards independence. Control can show itself as overt force. This usually results in intimidation or threats towards the teenager or young adult. Sometimes a simple step towards the child is enough to remind them of unpleasant incidents from years ago. This type of action retards a young adult's ability to adjust to independent life from a fear of reprisal and the child may fear leaving home, so they remain financially dependent for years to come.

As parents we can control using our financial resources to get our children to do what we want. If the only way we can get our kids together is by paying for a family vacation, then we are really controlling our children with money. Parents who reward their children with money are really building a relationship built on a financial exchange. Monetary relationships replace the emotional relationship that existed with your young child.

Financial blackmail can begin with the best of intentions. I know a woman whose father bought her a house—the house had to be close to where he lived. Unfortunately, this was a long way from the city centre and in a suburban neighbourhood of mostly young families. As a result the woman's social life deteriorated and her sole consistent relationship was with her father. The bond was so close that when he remarried, she was not allowed to stay in his home when she visited because of the disruption she caused with her stepmother. She stayed at a nearby hotel and, now in her fifties, still lives in the house her father bought for her. Her father died but she has not established or maintained another relationship in her life.

Feigning helplessness is another way to manipulate children into complying with your wishes. A comment like, "I'm looking after my sick father. Why can't you be there to help me?" causes a child to worry about a parent's ability to cope and so he/she remains in the family home. Usually this pattern starts when the children are much younger, and the child frequently ends up missing school. The child is less financially independent because of their inability to maintain a job. Frequent absences cause a very poor employment record, keeping them in their parent's house longer.

Ultimately, loyalty to the family may be the key motivating force to help maintain control over a young adult. This often happens when a teenager meets a girlfriend or boyfriend and the relationship is getting serious. Jealousy can develop if the teen is spending more time with the new partner and his or her family. Parents can feel displaced by this new interest in their child's life. There is a desperate attempt to maintain contact by providing financial assistance but, it is at this point that the emotional connection is replaced by one that centres around financial assistance. Family visits focus on business or financial exchanges to spend time with the young adult who falls into a pattern of financial dependency; the financial obligations of the parents can escalate rapidly.

Guilt

How many of us make parental decisions based on guilt as opposed to sound parental judgement? That guilt can stem from a variety of reasons: disappointment over what your son or daughter has made of his or her life, a divorce that separated you from your children, a job that limits your time with your children, and unrealistic expectations for your child. All of these reasons can cause us to provide unnecessary financial assistance to our children.

With guilt directing the relationship, you can be certain that your children will pick up on it and use it to their advantage. The financial assistance you will provide will always be used up and never be enough. Your child might well grow up to be constantly asking for more even when you have no more money available. With wealthier families the amount of money required could be extensive, with a fortune being squandered on questionable habits, activities, and shady investments.

Obsessive Love

Sometimes a parent's love is so all-consuming that they use money to keep their children in their lives because they feel heartbroken when their child stays away for any length of time. Money is the only tool they can use to keep their child close. It was a security blanket to maintain peace with their child when he or she was a young child. The child only learned to respond to financial demonstrations instead of emotional support.

It is precisely this learned behaviour that deprives parents of the love they crave. The financial transaction that replaced emotional support means that young adults look for the payoff when they are with their parents. It can be as simple as money to buy airplane tickets to come and visit, or it may be a request for a down-payment on a condominium. But it may grow into a relentless demand for regular payouts to meet their everyday financial commitments.

Like all parents they have a need to provide financial support throughout their children's upbringing; they want them to be happy. Unlike many parents though, they believe that supplying them with a personal line of credit is the answer. The difficulty comes when the line of credit outgrows the parents' ability to pay. At this point both children and parents are at a loss because the foundation of their relationship—the financial support—is no longer available.

What Will Everyone Think?

Believe it or not, there are parents who insist that their children keep the secret that they are not financially secure. Whatever the reason, the image of struggling to make it is not something these parents want their children to be sharing with others. So these parents will continue to prop their children up financially—forever.

And how long can it take? Well, for some children it can take a lifetime. For them, there is very little consequence to spending excessive amounts of cash because Mom and Dad are always there to top up the bank account. Eventually your child might have a family of his or her own and, as the parent of that child, you will continue to feel responsible for all the bills in that household as well.

I've seen the results of this type of thinking for years. Some children go on living in the role for years, never really accomplishing anything with their lives. I've seen older adults who live on a parental allowance all of their lives. I've seen children of wealthy parents borrow constantly to maintain the lifestyle of their new family, including a spouse and grandchildren.

One father I knew was obsessed with keeping up appearances in his town for both himself and his children. They always had the latest and the best of everything, despite the fact that the father had financial difficulties compounded by a gambling habit. Eventually the debts grew too large to handle, the father was overcome with helplessness and killed himself and his grown children.

Summary

Despite the messages that our children pick up from society about the need to have everything, as parents our needs can drive children into a financially dependent lifestyle. It is absolutely necessary to understand our own motives to change a pattern of behaviour that may have been going on for years. The financially dependent lifestyle has been supported and encouraged by all the players in the relationship. For any of the players— the parents—to implement change they need to examine and understand why they have been partners in this.

Once that has been achieved it is possible to make changes in the parent-child relationship. The only way to break free of the financial dependency is to feel secure in your own feelings towards your child. The sooner you deal with your own feeling of insecurity, the sooner you will be able to deal with your children, regardless of their age. Those feelings should include a love that promotes confidence in your emotional relationship with your child, and a belief that your child has the ability to succeed independent of your financial support.

Key Points
- Parents enable the dependency because of their own emotional needs.
- When the time comes independence must to be celebrated by parents and child together.
- Control is how parents actually keep their children dependent.
- Fear, guilt and love make saying no to financial demands by children very difficult for parents.
- Keeping up appearances is often a motivator for continually providing for children beyond reason.

9. Learning to Deal With Your Feelings

Coping with a son or daughter who is making increased demands on your financial resources can be extremely stressful. They need to understand the message from their parents that the bank machine is no longer handing out withdrawals but that it could open for deposits. Chances are that deposits are never going to happen, but if you can stop the dependency you can assure your own peace of mind about your own assets. You will also be able to take pleasure in the knowledge that your child will undoubtedly be better off as an individual.

We walk a fine line when it comes to helping support a child in a time of real need. At what point do we cross the line and develop the dependent relationship? It is never tangible until we acknowledge we are uncomfortable with the ongoing demands. And it is precisely then that you must do something about straightening out the situation or the demands will escalate and they might spiral out of control.

Most parents want to help their child to a reasonable degree. But what is reasonable? It will have a lot to do with your own financial status and values. However, unreasonable demands on your bank account and emotional well-being can be extremely difficult in any socio-economic group. A cell phone for a teenager is unreasonable if there is barely enough income to pay the rent; a car for a teenager is unreasonable and unnecessary if the cost is tapping into retirement savings.

Assistance should be gladly offered when the need is clear and it helps the child move towards independence. Money for school supplies or books is a great way to support children who are attempting to further their education. Money given to a child to go out and party with friends is not a productive use of limited funds—the child must learn to plan for special events. This may involve learning about the concept of saving.

Harnessing Your Love

The number one reason that we are motivated to over-indulge our children is our undying love for them. It is the first emotion that compels us to support them in their times of need. It is also the emotion that works against us when we try to limit the dependency that has expanded out of control.

Learning to accept the fact that your love for your child will remain intact despite the financial transaction is crucial. Love can also be shown simply in the joy you feel and share with your child at their own successes and individual achievements throughout life's many milestones. A parent's love for his or her child transcends good and bad times and is not defined by the quantity of things that have been given to that child.

Giving when it is unnecessary is simply an extension of your love for your child. The act of giving is not what defines your love for a son or daughter. The love you have for your children should not and cannot be described or defined through the purchase of a cell phone or car. The need to give starts with the need we have to be able to provide for and protect our children, which is undying.

Over time, if we are not able to control our love and put limits on what we provide for our children, we create a child who becomes increasingly dependent. Our love must also recognize the need for our children to grow up to be independent adults. These adults will eventually have families and have the need, themselves, to help their children grow up to be independent. We must be able to harness our love and recognize that a cycle of giving is separate from the love that we have for our children. The inability to stop the cycle of dependency will have long term negative effects on the whole family.

At what point is the need to give a substitute for the love that we are unable to express in any other way? Have many of our children grown up defining how much we love them by the number of things that we give them? I hope not many. And finally, it is because our love is so powerful that we are most vulnerable to being so hurt!

Living with Fear

There are always signs that the situation with your child has deteriorated regardless of their age. You realize that you are being used more and more frequently by your children to maintain their fantasy lifestyle. It is the realization of the many forms of manipulation that a child of any age might use to get the necessary funds. It can cause undue long-term stress in your life and inevitably, if the demands become more frequent or outrageous, fear begins to creep into your thoughts. These thoughts focus on both your own financial security and the well-being of your child.

Another sign might be that you are constantly giving to your child and eventually their friends jump on the bandwagon, so they are constantly eating at your house or you are always driving them around the neighbourhood. You have little time for yourself—both in your free time and in your own home, and your financial resources and your personal freedom are sacrificed.

In this above situation you are lucky if your child has the ability to choose friends carefully. I have had parents describe to me how their home was taken over by their child's acquaintances and then cleaned out of all jewellery and electronic equipment. These friends he had met at the mall were pawning the goods to buy drugs.

Another signal occurs when your child, regardless of age, is always making requests, even demands, for money. With younger children the demands are for things that they would like to do or buy—when a new movie comes out or new running shoes are needed. As they get older the needs are greater, but the reasons for the need becomes less clear. The demands increase until you realize that you are subsidizing a lifestyle with hundreds of your dollars every month.

Manipulation is another indicator that you are being taken for a sucker. When an adult child tells you that they don't have enough money for food for the third time that month you know something is not right. It might be that the child is having a rough time with work, but it is rather suspicious when the child is working three different jobs. Addictions have a way of taking everything a person has along with everything of those around that person. It is terrifying to know that you are dealing with an addict, and often impossible to understand. Addicts live to feed the addiction and have little concern for those they use to satisfy their need.

One of the ultimate fears when you are confronted with the reality of providing too much of a good thing to your child is when you disagree with your spouse about that reality and how to deal with it. At this point your marriage is in jeopardy because of the nature of your relationship with your child and your spouse. To determine how to bring order back into the relationship with your child, as parents you both will have to work together on a unified strategy. Failure to do that will alienate you from each other, communication will break down, and your child will have easier access to one of you. This can only lead to an increase in manipulation by your child.

Coping with Guilt

Another fear is of being alienated from a child who has grown used to automatically being given the things that he/she requests. The reality of saying no will have consequences. Often an adult child or young adult child will punish his parents for refusing to pay up. The addict who just needs forty dollars for groceries gets tiresome after repeated requests. The I just need line comes up as often as Could I borrow…?

The trouble with persistent demands is that you will inevitably have to say no at some point. Each of us draws our own line, but there is always the underlying fear that your child will resent you for taking a stand. You end up on the receiving end of the silent treatment from your child. This means that, unlike before, when they were in touch constantly, they are now nowhere to be found. The phone just isn't ringing like it once was and you are tempted to phone—sometimes you do but get no response. You are being punished by your child for finally standing your ground and resisting his or her demands. This silent treatment may sound childish, but it is very stressful, particularly if you are used to regular contact with your child. This adult is trying to make you feel uncomfortable with your decision. By not knowing where he/she is, you begin to think that something might be wrong. Guilt begins to creep into your thoughts for refusing to cooperate with the financial request and you convince yourself that you are at fault for not supporting your child when he/she needed you. So, even though your child made an inappropriate demand and then refused to maintain contact, the pressure tactic has worked because you have convinced yourself that you are to blame.

Guilt will almost always win out over what is reasonable in any given circumstance and cause you to relent and give in to the demands. This guilt is not new; it is precisely the same guilt that has caused you to give in to your child for years. It is the overriding feeling that has pushed this child/parent relationship to this level of transactions with your child. Your moments together are usually built around you providing money for one reason or another. It is hard to acknowledge when this relationship begins because you are usually so thankful for the time with your child that you forget that the contact is made only when you have agreed to pay out!

Eventually parents will have to develop more control of the new pattern in the relationship that is being established. Actions will have to be meaningful for the message to be delivered effectively. There can be no backing down from positions that protect your own financial interests, so it is imperative that the correct action be taken for the relationship to be re-established on solid footing.

Key Points

- A child's over-dependence rather than independence is a product of how well his or her parents' have managed to walk that line to maintain their peace of mind.
- It is only natural that parents want to assist their children.
- Wealthy, as well as working class, parents are at risk of having dependent adult children.
- Misguided love can be the number one reason why certain children grow up to become dependent adults.
- Love does not have to be shown only through financial assistance.
- Demands from children can become more frequent and outrageous, and this is cause for concern.
- Pay close attention to how funds are being used and who your child is hanging out with.
- When making decisions concerning giving assistance to your child, make sure that you and your spouse agree on the plan of action.
- The feeling of guilt makes it much more difficult to say no.
- Be prepared for the silent treatment when you don't fully cooperate with your child's demands.

10. Taking Action

Once you decide to take action it is important to understand the various options that are available to you. Consistency and determination to break your child's pattern of dependency will be necessary. A change in your behaviour will certainly be noticed by your child, regardless of his or her age. You will have to be intuitive enough to try and understand how this new reality will be dealt with. Regardless of whether you decide you can no longer make the cell phone payments for your teenager or you are no longer paying for extravagant family vacations, the reactions will be similar. Your child will feel that you are depriving them of something they should have. It may also be that they believe they have a right to these things!

The ways we over-indulge our children vary, so too will the need to alter the strategies we use to stop the dependency. Without a doubt, the ability to just say no will go a long way to stopping the never-ending cycle. Going cold turkey, although the most effective method, is not always possible when life-long habits of indulging are in place. It is within the realm of possibility that a child of any age who is told no will express a wide range of emotions. An adult with an addiction, for example, might be dangerous if they are told that you are no longer going to feed their habit. A teenager who wants a cell phone may call you every name in the book. A younger child could have a tantrum and embarrass you in front of a whole store. Children who are used to getting the things they want will have great difficulty dealing with the new you. Everyone is different, but tread softly if you fear the worst, particularly if you fear for your safety.

Become more Evasive

When children are asking, demanding, implying, insisting, or thinking they should be given something, they are attempting to elicit a response from us. Of course, the ideal response they want to hear is that we agree with their needs assessment. Unfortunately many of us feel compelled to respond to this immediately, which is not at all necessary. We need to take time to process what we are being asked for.

A busy lifestyle, guilt feelings, love, and fear often cause us to give in immediately to these requests. Our children need to understand that we need time to consider our responses rather than submitting to them blindly. They also need to know that the answer may not always be the answer they want. This is important life-long training for them. It teaches them that there are things that don't always work out. There will always be things we want but don't need, that we can't have.

How can a parent develop this new more evasive style and get away from the bank machine definition? Quite simply, you must slow the whole process down. You can take control by not specifically answering the request at all. A good tactic would be to ask your child questions why he or she needs such a thing, and put the child in a more defensive mode. Another tactic would be to comment that you really don't believe the item he or she is requesting is that good, and then quote a newspaper article that states that the item is a waste of money. Their request may continue but their position has become more restricted and you are countering without giving in immediately.

Remember, your child now must convince you because you have the power to grant his or her request. By not giving in immediately your child may now be more willing to listen to you. It's like money in the bank!

Be Discreet

Sometimes our openness with our children leaves us vulnerable to their expectations. I remember a time as a teenager when I used to visit a girlfriend's house. Occasionally at dinner she would ask her father how much money he made. His reply was simply "That's really not your business." Looking back on this, I realize that he was probably right. This is particularly true if we know we have children who would love to get their hands on some of our hard-earned money.

Being more discreet about income leaves more opportunity to discuss financial responsibilities. The focus then switches from discretionary income to expenses that are incurred monthly. Parents who are successful at limiting hand-outs to children often emphasize on-going monthly expenses. They may be perfectly capable of paying for some toy that a teenager wants, but the teenager is now reluctant to ask because he has just heard that the electricity bill for the past month was three hundred dollars. The fact that the teenager has that information is more likely to stop him or her from requesting some other item.

Without having specific knowledge about what your income is, but knowing what some of your expenses are, a parent is in an easier position to say no to a child. The request may still come from the child despite their knowledge but the difference lies in their response to the no. A teenager who understands that your debt load may be too heavy is more amenable to backing off on the request. As a parent you may be managing your finances quite well but now your teenager may only be aware of the daunting monthly bills you pay. It's a reality check that you can hold for insurance purposes should you decide to say no to the request.

Don't always feel you have to share your spending habits with your children. They don't always have to know how much you paid for that antique item you just bought or for the car you recently leased. For some it just demonstrates that you have money to spend but it is not being spent on them. I've occasionally bought antiques at garage sales or auctions and my kids never noticed them until they had already been in the house for months. At that point, I would simply state that I've had the pieces for months. They may not respond or they may ask how much it cost. Rather than say it is not their business, I say that it was an amazing deal!

Older children might be bold enough to question some of your spending habits, particularly if they are things that are of interest to you. If you enjoy doing home decorating as I do, you may get a comment that you spend too much time or money on that hobby or interest. You might feel compelled to defend, or feel guilty about, indulging your interests, but do not give in to either of these feelings. Celebrate your interests as long as they are productive and healthy. I've also pointed out to my children that I've worked for over thirty years and I can spend my money on the things that interest me! There is no need for further discussion on this matter, and it is not something you have to go to great lengths to explain.

Use Community Resources

If you have teenagers and young adults who are constantly requesting things, but are not willing to help themselves, it is probably better to steer them in the right direction instead of agreeing to their demands. Your community almost always has a wealth of resources at your disposal. By using these resources you can help your child reach out and help them to relate more closely to their community, promote greater independence, and improve their self-esteem.

When my daughter was seventeen and needed more money we did not have to look further than the local mall. Through her step-brother she landed a job in the mall information booth. This part-time position kept her happy for several years. It taught her about responsibility and developed many of the office and public relations skills she uses today, while providing her with the spending money she needed for the lifestyle she wanted while she was a student. This was a tremendous help to her mother and me.

Use the newspaper to find out about activities for children the same age as your own. Sometimes there are articles that can inform you about what you should be expecting from your children at their age. And, if you are really lucky, you might find an article illustrating a point you have been trying to make with your teenager and give it to him or her to read. There is nothing like having a credible reference to back up your perspective in a difference of opinion you have been having with your child. I'm constantly cutting out newspaper clippings and leaving them around the house!

The local library offers all kinds of resources to help you deal with children of all ages. If you are looking for examples of role models for your children and you don't have many people to turn to, the library is the place to go. There are endless articles and books on specific issues related to parenting. And don't forget the Internet, you can use it for research to make your point as well!

Lean on Friends

Friends are a great resource to help you control the hemorrhaging from your bank account that your children caused. Chances are that many of them have lived through similar circumstances and can relate to what you are experiencing. Some of them may have experience in education, psychology, or finance that they can bring to the table when they are listening to you.

You really need friends who are willing to listen to the issues that you are experiencing before they tell you what to do. Make sure that you are clear about not only the extreme demands by your child, but also your anxiety. You can't have one without the other until you have decided on a course of action and are ready to deal with the fallout. Friends can offer you the support you will need to break the existing pattern of dependency with your child. If this dependency is in an advanced stage it will not disappear easily and for every two steps forward you take holding your ground, a dependent young adult will increase the pressure with more extreme stories about why he/she needs more money. I knew one mother who finally had to admit to herself that the stories were getting too bizarre—her son asked for money for cancer treatments and for her to make a cheque out to a doctor and mail it. The address belonged to a friend of her son's who was going to cash the cheque. Her son was an addict. It was finally time for her to say, No more!

The sad thing about this lady was her extreme guilt when she said no to her son. Her friends could see the conflict between love and guilt within her but not everyone is capable of understanding that battle. Surround yourself with people who can empathize with this inner turmoil while encouraging you to hold your ground. With this type of support it is possible to change the dependency cycle.

Alternative Ways to Give

It is important not to give in to the I just need... request each time it comes up. Think carefully about why the request is being made and whether it is necessary. These I just need... requests for money can put a serious dent in your bank account in short order. Don't be too quick to give in to the requests because the more you give the easier it becomes for your child to continue to ask for more money.

You do have alternatives if you want to continue to help your child but doubt that the money is being put to good use. Rather than giving an adult child money for food, consider making a meal for your son or daughter to take home. Offer to buy groceries to see if the need is real. If the money is for something other than what was stated then your offer to help may be objected to or refused.

Cars are often used as a reason for needing extra money, particularly if they are needed for work. Someone who isn't looking after the thing they need to work is usually spending money on the wrong things. Drugs, alcohol, and gambling cause insatiable demands on even the largest of incomes. If you suspect your money has been diverted to one or more of these addictions consider other ways to help out. By sending your adult child to your garage to have their car repairs done will ensure that the money is used for the intended repair.

If you feel you have to co-sign a loan to help your child get out of debt, remember that you are actually insuring that you will pay off the loan should your child default. Consider a private meeting with the manager or the loans officer at your financial institution to arrange for the bank to deduct the loan payments at source from your child's paycheque. In addition, check to see if it is possible for the bank to agree to pay down outstanding loans directly. That way at least any further default on payments can be avoided.

Protect yourself, have an attorney draw up legal papers to verify that you have either given or loaned a child a specified amount of money. These papers can be voided should the money be repaid. If the money isn't repaid, then it can be deducted from the estate after your death. This will allow your other children to have their equal share of your estate and eliminate the resentment towards the sibling who may have been extra needy.

Remember that whatever you offer may not be enough. The sad reality of an addict is that you are feeding the addiction—not your child. You may constantly say to yourself that your son or daughter is standing right in front of you but you don't know him or her anymore. It is extremely difficult to relate to an addict because addicts only care about satisfying their addiction. An addict doesn't care whether there is money left in your bank account at the end of the day because they prefer to have that money from the account to feed their habit!

Seek Counselling

If you are frightened about the endless demands for money and the unhealthy dependency between you and your child then it may be time to seek counselling for a situation that you are not able to deal with alone. Friends probably cannot offer you the concrete steps you need to take to stop the dependency.

Counselling can give you an ongoing outlet to express your frustration because a dependent adult child can make monetary demands anytime. Counsellors can provide you with the tools you need to respond to those demands more effectively. You don't need to suffer in your fear or guilt alone. Share these feelings with a professional to remove some of the burden from your shoulders.

Get a Life, Get Busy and Get Away

If your life has become sedentary you are a much more obvious target for a child who is trying to dip into your savings. Are you at your home waiting to hear from that child who is constantly making increasingly large demands on your bank account? If that is the case, you have a big target in the middle of your forehead that says "hit me".

You need to establish other relationships and activities in your life outside of the one you have with your child. This is particularly true if you no longer have children at home and have free time. Join a fitness club or take up card playing to get out of the house. Take up a hobby that consumes your free time and takes you out of the house. Not only does this take your mind off your demanding child, but it also gives him or her the message that there are other things in your life besides him or her.

Consider treating yourself to a vacation or two with

friends. If you are now alone, why not consider going away for an extended period of time? This creates a physical distance between you and your child and gives you freedom to live the life you deserve. It also allows your adult child the opportunity to get back on his or her feet without depending on you.

It is important to maintain a life for yourself rather than waiting to live through your children. Spending family time with your child is great, but not if it increases the stress in your life. You are not responsible for the unreasonable needs of a grown child and his or her family. Your love for this child, and possibly grandchildren, will bring tremendous turmoil into your home when unrealistic demands come your way. You need to be able to walk away, at least temporarily, and accept that meeting these demands is no longer your responsibility.

The Intervention

If you are faced with a dysfunctional teenager, young adult, or adult child who is living way out of control, it could eventually lead to the time when you want to do an intervention. An intervention can be held at your house and will inevitably involve the people close to the child who is out of control. They will share both their concerns and their love for the person, while demanding a behavioural change.

Usually the intervention presents a united front from all involved, but it is made clear that the individual must comply with the demands to ensure continued support. It can be a life-changing event or a very traumatic experience, depending on the outcome. Usually a third party is helpful to guide the intervention and to maintain a positive tone during the proceedings. The parent, when considering an intervention, must acknowledge that the situation with the child is dire and needs outside help.

Become a Minimalist or Move

If your child refuses to take the hints and continues to make demands on you while criticizing your lifestyle, consider becoming a minimalist. Many people are getting into minimalism in their homes, and it can release you from the extra baggage you have been keeping around your house. It sends a clear message that you have decided to live a lean lifestyle with few extra luxuries.

You can use the opportunity to explain to your dependent child that you are cutting back to have smaller monthly expenses. Explain that you can no longer afford to live as you did before. Be discreet but make it clear that you have a limited budget, you can not live extravagantly and that it is important for you to control your spending to maintain the quality of life you have been accustomed to living. A smaller home means that there won't be room for adult children who want to remain living in the household. You may need assistance to help you make this transition, but once you free yourself from the burden of caring for adult children your own standard of living will improve. Counselling can help you deal with the emotional trauma of separating yourself from your children for the first time.

Minimalism gives your child of any age a visual indication that you are streamlining. It can be seen as a concrete effort to save money on living expenses. It also provides you with a reason when you feel it is necessary to say no to financial demands. It is easier to say no when you have taken steps yourself to save money on expenses. It's always easier to explain saving on expenses because you don't want to point out to a dependent child that you want to put money away into your savings. In this situation less is better; so don't volunteer more information than is necessary because it could come back to haunt you later.

Some parents might want to create more space between themselves and their children. There can be many reasons for moving that don't have to be directly tied into dependent children; you might be moving closer to friends or other relatives. The need to find work is another possibility, as is seeking better health care facilities. Moving allows you to re-establish your life as an independent adult without grown-up children regularly sapping your financial resources. It is a drastic measure, obviously, but against some of the unrealistic demands that are placed on you, it may be necessary.

Make Parameters Clear

It is crucial to set the parameters very early in your child's life so they understand what is acceptable when requesting funds for something. As they get older their needs will change but the parameters must remain constant. If a child has learned that having a tantrum when they don't get the toy by the time they are five does not work, chances are they are not going to have a fit when you refuse to get them a cell phone as a teenager. They need to know that there are limits to your financial resources and that everyone in the family is affected by them.

If possible, provide your child or teenager with options for obtaining some of the things he or she wants. Maybe Christmas is just a few months away and it could be their gift. For a teenager, maybe someone in the neighbourhood is willing to pay to have work done. Alternatives to providing their every want are possible, if you take the time to consider them.

Be clear about what your income is used for without providing too many details. Emphasize, without over-explaining, that your budget doesn't allow for many extras. A child will always point to the flaws in that argument—particularly if you are extravagant in your own spending.

Make expectations about part-time jobs for teenagers and young adults clear. They should use their money to pay for the things that they want. Monthly payments are not smart unless and until they have shown an ability to save for a rainy day should they lose their job. Putting money away for schooling should be emphasized to help establish good saving habits. Money earned is not just for spending on a fantasy lifestyle. Some of it needs to be put aside for real-life issues.

Young adults who are still living at home need to contribute to the household. It is imperative that they pay monthly rent to get into the habit of paying bills regularly. Rent for payment of household expenses should be a given once a job is secured. You are not looking for permanent boarders in your home. You want your children to leave eventually feeling secure in their ability to manage their own expenses. Having children live at home with no financial responsibilities is only doing them a disservice.

In Conclusion

Without a doubt taking action requires a commitment to deal with the emotional drain that will result from confronting pretty stiff resistance. It will require careful planning, support, and a strategy to facilitate the change needed to help your child become an independent adult, and allow you to live a more independent life as well. Always remember that you are doing your child a favour by enabling him or her to function without your ongoing financial support. Failure to stop an unchecked run on your bank account only increases the dependency over time. It can also place you in a precarious financial situation.

Key Points

- Parents need to consciously change the way they respond to demands from their children and maintain a consistent position.
- Results of refusing to cooperate may be erratic as children adjust to a change in a lifelong habit of dependency.
- Take the time to process demands prior to responding.
- Resist the temptation to give in immediately.
- Regardless of age, children need to know that we don't always get the answer we want.
- By not giving in to a demand you force your child to listen to you because you control the purse strings.
- Don't share financial information unless absolutely necessary.
- Rely on outside resources to solve problems instead of using your bank account as the solution.
- Talk to friends who can be supportive of your concerns about your overly dependent children.
- If you must intervene, help out by giving something else instead of money.
- When the situation becomes desperate, seek

professional help.

• Involve yourself in things that put meaning into your life as an individual.

• Bring concerned family members together to share their concerns with your dependent child.

• Make yourself scarcer by planning things like an extended vacation.

• Set parameters so that your child knows that there are limitations to your response to their demands.

11. How to Deal with Specific Demands

We are sometimes caught off guard by the unexpected demands from our children. There is no way to predict the exact financial demands that our children will make, but there are some common ones that are ongoing. These are the tried and true perceived needs of many teenagers, young adults and adult children; the demands will vary depending on what stage they are at in their life and how dependent or independent they have become. All represent potential bottomless pits in terms of lost savings for a parent. Your child's intentions for repayment may be sincere but the reality may be completely different.

Cell Phones

Any parent with a teenager knows about the dependency many of them have on cell phones. It is no exaggeration to say that many teenagers and young adults feel naked, if not helpless, without one. This is the generation who use cell phones to stay in contact with everyone every minute of the day. This is not using the cell phone for emergencies, but as a way to keep up with every one of his or her friends on a non-stop basis.

The truth is that many of us have been burned by our teenagers' huge cell phone bills. We buy these things to keep in contact with our children only to find that we can't reach them because they are constantly on the phone with their friends. The monthly bill then skyrockets because of long distance charges, text messaging and conference calling.

If you are concerned about keeping in touch with your child here are some things to remember. At school, if there is an emergency, your child wil be allowed to phone you on a school phone. Schools do not allow students to use cell phones in the school building. So if your child has one, chances are he or she is going to leave the school to make calls to other kids who should be in school.

In the evening an alternative to having a cell phone is calling you from wherever he or she is and giving you the phone number—then your child is a little less mobile than if he or she has a cell. Today, knowing where your child is can be a much safer thing than them having a cell phone. If your child is out for long periods during the day then a cell phone may offer comfort, but read and understand the plan before signing on the dotted line. Before getting a cell phone for your son or daughter consider the following:

- Just say no!
- Don't sign up for a plan.
- If you have a cell phone, lend it to your teenager.
- Know the phone numbers of the places where your child is visiting.
- If possible, drive your child to and from events.
- Tell your teenager they need to get a job first.
- Your child should save a year of rental money prior to the purchase of a plan.
- If a phone is purchased, buy a monthly number of minutes and set the maximum amount available in advance.

- Cell phones cause one of the biggest disturbances in schools because of students who can't do without them.
- Many teenagers grow up safely without them and still remain in contact with their parents.
- You are not depriving your child of anything that he or she can't survive without.

Entertainment Requirements

Our children have far more options for entertainment than have ever existed in the past. Total entertainment movie complexes provide an array of activities—from eating a meal to actually seeing the movie all under one roof. Other activities make the movie mega-complex a haven for teens to hang out together.

Many young adults go to a club or local bar on a regular basis. Then there are sporting events. These activities can cost a lot of money, and your children may have difficulty saying no if friends are all going. Mom and Dad, or both, are the bad guys if they cannot participate. They never consider the fact that they have already spent their money for that particular week.

- If a request comes to you, just say no!
- Remind your child that they have already spent their allowance.
- If they are working part-time, tell your teenager to wait until their next paycheque.
- Mention that you already spent your entertainment budget for the week.
- Remember, an advance on their allowance is a line of credit and you may not want them getting used to

that concept.

• Get the message across at as young an age as possible that they have to live within their means.

The Internet

I use the term Internet loosely because it is the real reason why our children want computers in their bedrooms. I could have said computer, but it is the Internet that our children want access to. We may agonize for days, weeks or months over what computer to buy, but it is the Internet that can be used to expose your child to anything with just a touch on the keyboard. Once the Internet hook-up has been installed in a child's room, you have opened the gateway for him or her to far more fascinating things than are going on in your house.

I have known teenagers and young adults to park themselves in their rooms for hours on end avoiding any interaction with family members. They can become so addicted to Internet use that they keep erratic hours and sleep patterns become disturbed. Along with the added monthly expense comes a decrease in family exchanges as the child becomes one with the Internet.

Internet expenses can be minimal if you restrict the expense to the monthly line connection expense. If you are attaching another line to another computer your expenses can be significant. Then if your child starts e-gambling or e-purchasing, your expenses can explode. For many people it is just unthinkable to give in to the demand for a separate computer for the bedroom. For parents who can afford the line they might reconsider, if they knew what they were exposing their child to. Consider the following when you hear such a request:

- Just say no!
- Tell the child he or she will have to save the money for the computer and the Internet fees.
- If your child won't stay off the Internet, put the computer in a locked room and control access to it.
- Have a family computer in a common place with one Internet hook-up.
- Keep the computer in a high traffic area of the house.
- Restrict use to certain hours of the day.
- Restrict the amount of time that your child can spend on the computer.
- If possible, buy software that doesn't allow access to certain sites.(i.e. porn, gambling).
- Buy anti-virus software since teenagers have a knack for downloading all kinds of viruses that could mean expensive service calls.

Electronic Gadgets (Grown-up Toys)

As was stated earlier, our children's taste in their toys gets more sophisticated as they age. An important rule of thumb is to remember when they were little and received all those presents at birthdays and Christmas. That's right; they generally played with one thing—quite possibly the cheapest toy in the lot. The rest of the stuff cluttered up your house and every inch of closet space. Well, as they get older the toys get more expensive, and they can still be found all over the house. There is no end to their taste for DVDs and CDs. iPods and Palm Pilots are a must because they are the things to have. Many of these devices duplicate each other and the memory is far greater than your child will ever need to pass a grade ten math class. Electronic machines of every imaginable shape and size can take over your home at a rapid rate, and you won't have any idea what they are used for. The ones listed above are some of the cheaper toys, I haven't even mentioned the plasma televisions, new cell phones, and digital recording devices. As I said, those back-to-school specials are not like the old days! All of these things can be a huge drain on your bank account. Keep things simple and don't give into demands that grow as technology changes. A friend I had in my twenties spent close to two thousand dollars for one of the first VCR machines. It was a waste of money just to be the first to have a future outdated electronic component. Consider the following before giving into the lure of the electronic playground:

- Just say no!
- Answer: We don't need it.
- State: We can't really afford it at this time.
- Comment: When you are working you can buy these things.
- Say, in a matter of fact manner: I have an oil bill to pay!
- Tell him or her: When you have the money saved, you can buy it!
- Say: I'll gladly put the money you earn each week-end away so you can buy this one day.

Designer Clothes

We have all somewhat bought into the notion that fashion is an important part of who we are. We act like sheep lined up at the clothes counter buying the latest fashion trends for our children whatever their ages. Today even babies are indulged with designer clothes which cost a small fortune, even though they are going to outgrow them within a few months. We are all to blame for our children wanting designer clothes when they don't have the income to afford them.

Fashion can change dramatically from one year to the next and tastes in clothes can fluctuate depending on who the current role models for our children are. Dressing your children, at any age, can cost a small fortune so the challenge is to limit the expense, keep the peace at home and convince your child that he or she still looks great. They won't take your opinion on that! Here are some things you can do that might help when confronted with the demand to purchase high-priced clothing:

- Just say no!
- Ask your child how many items similar to the one he or she wants are scattered in his or her room.
- Ask him or her how much money has been saved toward the piece of clothing.
- Tell your teenager you need to see a price comparison from at least three stores.
- Take your child to a discount clothing outlet to see if they have a similar item at a cheaper price.
- I'm only willing to pay this amount… is a good response.
- I just heard that people are no longer buying those! really throws them for a loop.

Vacations

More and more young people are travelling further and further to see sporting events or lie on a beach somewhere.

There are also special school trips, particularly in high school graduation year. Because these happen when they are still in school teenagers probably cannot afford the expense.

The result is that parents often face the dilemma about what to do under tremendous pressure for school trips in particular. Many of us decide to pay for these trips because they are with school but it is important for our teenagers and young adults to take some financial responsibility for these trips.

Usually high school and college trips are planned years in advance. This gives everyone a warning to plan for the costs. You could find yourself paying for exotic trips for your child to places you have never gone to yourself. Don't let this happen!

Impulsive unexpected trips planned by friends can also come up. The excitement of going away often over-shadows the fact that your child probably does not have enough money to pay for the trip. You get the picture. Here are some things you can do to keep some money in your pocket for your own vacation:

- Just say no!
- Find out about school trips well in advance.
- Encourage your teenager to open a bank account early for the planned trip.
- Your child can get a part-time job to pay for the trip. Then he or she can go.
- If you are willing to pay some of the cost, firmly state the amount and don't alter your commitment.
- If you decide to make a loan, write out the payment schedule and get your child's signature on it.
- Give your teenager or young adult a breakdown of

the total cost for any planned trip so they understand their financial commitment.

• If they have planned their own trip, have them come up with alternative packages or destinations to make price comparisons.

Buying a Car

Unless you are independently wealthy, buying a car is a financial drain on anyone's budget if kids are still in school or unemployed. The expenses tied into buying a vehicle, whether new or second-hand, multiply rapidly for a teenager or young adult. The purchase or lease price, insurance, gas, and repairs become a huge financial drain. And I haven't even included the cost of accidents and traffic tickets!

You may have a teenager or young adult who is putting tremendous pressure on you to support the purchase of a vehicle. A vehicle for a child can add up to five hundred to a thousand dollars per month—a huge commitment that the average household cannot afford.

Part-time jobs are usually the clincher for most teenagers who now believe that they can afford to buy a car. Of course, if they lose that part-time job at the mall, the bills for the car will still keep coming in at a regular pace. And you know exactly who will get stuck with the bills!

Transportation is crucial for teenagers and young adults, particularly if they must travel long distances to go to work or school. The difficulty is compounded if you do not live near public transportation. It is further complicated if you do not have a car and cannot drive them to certain places. Here are some things you can do to help you save money when the car discussion takes place:

• Just say no!

- Ask you son or daughter how many thousands of dollars he or she has saved.
- Ask your child to tell you the kind of car they are interested in and then have him or her call an insurance company to find out the cost of the insurance.
- Tell your son or daughter you can't afford to help pay for the vehicle.
- Tell him or her they have to pay for their schooling first.
- Tell your son or daughter that you are only willing to pay for schooling.
- Make a list of the total monthly payments.
- Hand them a copy of the schedule for buses near your house.
- Tell your son or daughter that they need a license first.
- Agree to lend your car when it is available as long as they pay for the gas.

Over-Indulgence in Activities

A time comes in every child's life when you would hope they will recognize their strengths or limitations in terms of a favourite activity. This is particularly important if this activity requires large sums of your money. This returns us to the American Idol Syndrome I discussed earlier. These activities might include dance, theatre, singing and music lessons, or any other specialized activity.

Usually, a teenager or young adult who hangs on to the dream that they are going to make it with their limited talent is avoiding dealing with the realities of life. The more they delay the inevitable the more it costs you. Unfortunately, some people make their living by promoting these false hopes to young people— and refusing to continue to finance the activity makes you the bad guy.

Don't get me wrong—it is important to expose our children to a variety of activities when they are young. This is part of their learning process about who they are and how they fit in their environment. As they get older they can better understand their own abilities and what they would prefer to be doing. If maturation continues into their young adult years they are able to understand their own capabilities, the need to plan for the future, and the expense required to pursue their activity.

A parent should be happy to see their young adult child moving into a career path in a trade, college, or university. Only the most talented and committed of children will pursue an activity and excel at a competitive level. For these talented individuals there are elite programs and scholarships to make the financial burden less difficult. But I am really talking about the young person who refuses to recognize their limited talent and continues to make financial demands on your budget even when they could be working at least part-time. To make matters worse, they have given up almost everything else to concentrate on these vain hopes. It is with that in mind that I offer the following suggestions on how to stop the drain from your bank account:

- Just say no.
- Tell your child that you are no longer able to pay for the lessons.
- Inform this young adult that they need to get a part-time job to pay for the activity.
- Emphasize the talent needed to make a living in

this particular activity.

• Refrain from false praise that raises false hopes.

• Explain that your budget limitations cannot include the activity any longer.

• Tell your young adult that they will have to save the money in advance.

• Do not sign anything to guarantee payment assuming that your son or daughter will earn the money to pay for it.

• Get an independent professional to assess your son or daughter's talents.

Tuition

Tuition is always a tough issue to deal with because it is only natural that if we can afford to, then we would support post-secondary studies—but often the length of the program combined with the cost per year becomes daunting. The best way to avoid the crisis is to plan ahead and save for your child's education from the time they are young—not something that many parents can afford.

Parents who are better off financially are not always in the clear when it comes to difficulties around tuition, particularly when they recognize that they have a perennial student as a child. Think about the annual tuition fees and then add on several years to any program, the financial strain becomes difficult to take.

For some young adults staying in school longer is directly related to the financial support that they have come to expect. It's difficult for a parent to pull the plug on a worthwhile way to provide financial support. But campus life can get very comfortable after a while and the demands of the real world may not look too tempting for someone that has not had to pay for anything for years while at university. Your young adult child may be far more dependent than you might have imagined; some not so gentle pushing in the right direction may be necessary to get them to finally stand on their own two feet.

Many parents cannot afford to put their child through university, but it is important to emphasize to them that they can still attain their goals. I had to pay for my tuition and, although it was a struggle, I felt I had accomplished something special when I earned my first degree. I realized later that my parents had provided me with room and board and that was all they could afford to do for me at the time. Give your child emotional support and control your own fears, guilt, and love to help your child through his or her education, even if you are not able to offer financial support. Here are some tips to help parents deal with the tuition issue:

- Just say no!
- Make sure your child's academic expectations are realistic.
- Indicate the amount you might be able to contribute.
- Suggest that your child apply for a scholarship.
- Students can apply for student loans.
- Limit the number of years that they can expect financial help from you.
- Set expectations for acceptable academic performance.
- Pull the plug if your child is not performing up to expectations.
- Suggest a part-time job to help defray costs.
- Know your own financial limits and do not feel

guilty about not being able to pay for university.

• Encourage your child's educational dreams within realistic financial parameters for all concerned.

• Have meetings with your child to plan and work out different possibilities to help them reach their academic goals.

Credit/Debit Cards

If you really want to watch your money disappear faster than you can earn it, give your teenager or young adult your credit or debit card for a few hours. The whole idea of credit and what that means is conceptual in nature. I still can't figure out why parents do this and then are outraged when they open their bill at the end of the month. The idea of being able to buy something without money and not having to pay immediately is a far cry from the teenager who has to wait for his or her allowance for something they want. Young people need to be taught the concept of credit and interest rates. They probably shouldn't have access to credit cards until they have full-time employment but a student only has to step onto a college or university campus to be invited to obtain a credit card immediately.

An exception is an expensive item that is being purchased and your son or daughter is going to pick it up. You then lend the card with the clear understanding that it is only to be used for that particular purchase. If you trust your son or daughter and all goes well, then you have also given him or her a lesson about how to use credit. It can be explained that he or she, or even you, have the money in a savings account to pay the bill when it arrives. Maybe it was safer to use a card than to carry all that cash around.

Teenagers and young adults are easy prey to individuals

who may lack the funds that your child has access to. If your child has a credit card, it will soon come to the attention of all their friends. It takes a strong teenager to say no to friends, and some of them will eventually start making demands that your child may not be willing to refuse. Why put your child in that position? Here are some tips to help parents deal with this problem:

- Just say no!
- Use it as a learning opportunity, allowing a small purchase and seeing if the statement at the end of the month will be paid in full.
- Emphasize that it can cost them twenty to thirty percent more using credit than if they pay cash.
- Explain that if used effectively, a credit card can actually help your future credit rating.

Request to Co-Sign a Loan

As mentioned, one of the fastest ways to get into debt is to co-sign a loan for your child. This request can come at any age but more than likely he or she will be an adult. You have to remember that an adult who needs someone to co-sign usually has a bad credit rating. If your child has a bad credit rating it means that he or she has not been making payments on time, or is already in debt up to his or her eyeballs.

Any parent who co-signs a loan has to be fully prepared and financially able to pay back the full amount of the loan, since you become responsible for paying the loan. Then, when applying for credit for yourself, you must declare the loan that you co-signed as a debt that you are carrying. If you need a car loan, your available credit could be affected by the loan that you have co-signed for your child.

PHIL CLAVEL

Nevertheless, it probably is worthwhile to talk to your adult child about the loan. Probe, asking questions that give you information about what the loan is for and how it will be used. Try to get information about how your child is doing financially, and don't be afraid to admit that co-signing would be too much responsibility for you financially. Here are some specific tips to help you:

- Just say no!
- State that you need a loan yourself at that particular time.
- Make alternative suggestions to deter them from buying something like a new car at that time.
- Tell them about a place that is hiring part-time workers.
- Remember if you co-sign, you are ultimately responsible.
- If you insist on co-signing, go to your bank and deal with them directly.
- Avoid loan companies that charge exorbitant rates and come knocking at your door at all hours.
- Ask yourself if you really believe your child is going to repay the loan.
- Evaluate your own financial resources.

Co-Signing for an Apartment

Inevitably your child will want to move out of your home even though they are not quite ready financially. Children who do this want to assert their independence, often without realizing the financial ramifications of such a move. The potential landlord is also going to recognize your child's short-sightedness, so your child is going to ask you to co-sign. The key thing to remember here is that, if your child defaults on the rent, you are responsible for payment. You have to ask yourself whether you are able to pay for two places over an extended period of time. Like most parents, your answer is probably no.

- Just say no!
- Make sure the lease is by the month and not for a year or more.
- Your child should have all the necessary up-front money on his or her own first month payment, last month payment, damage deposit, and so forth.
- If you insist on co-signing, tell your child in advance that any money you might have to pay will have to be repaid.
- Never co-sign for an apartment thinking that you are not responsible for payment. Ultimately, the place is yours until the lease is finished.
- Remember, you are signing a legal document.

Summary

There is no end to the creativity our children display in finding ways to spend our money. The list could probably go on for many pages. The requests mentioned above are for things over and above the call of parental duty as far as our financial responsibility is concerned. It is inevitable that, as a parent, you feel obliged to contribute to some of these things, but it is also important to remember that you are not helping your child by not being able to say no. A reality of life is that children of all ages have to learn what the limits are on what they are able to do. Without limits, we end up with some of the characters I mentioned earlier as young adults and adult children. Take a closer look at how to handle some of those situations.

12. How to Deal With Specific Individuals

The people I am referring to are the chronic cases who have grown beyond their teenage years wanting or needing to continue to tap into your financial resources for a variety of reasons. This is disturbing to a parent whether or not you are able to support them financially. Wealthy parents whom I have talked with are no more pleased with their children in these situations than parents with fewer financial resources.

The biggest difference for parents lies in the quality of life they are able to have in terms of their own financial resources. Adult children tapping into a parent's limited resources put that parent's quality of life at risk but, although a minority, some of them just don't care. Maybe that indifferent attitude is the most helpful antidote for parents when responding to these needy adult children who come calling for handouts.

The Opportunist

The opportunist is going to want to join the party any time, particularly if there are freebies to be had. Just when you think you can get away or afford to do something, this adult child wants to join in—so long as you are paying. It may only be a minor annoyance that this person only shows up if you are willing to pay the tab, but if you have limited funds, then you can't look forward to that family gathering at a restaurant anymore because it costs you double.

The opportunist lives a little more freely in wealthy families because the financial drain doesn't affect the parents as dramatically. The resentment may come from other siblings who see their inheritance dwindling away. Parents may begin to feel resentment towards the adult child if the constant giving is taken for granted. When parents are on a limited budget, anything they give to the opportunist negatively affects another part of their lives. It may mean that there is not enough money to pay the bills or that there is more owed on the credit card at the end of each month. Either way, the brakes need to be applied so as to stop the dependency.

- Don't offer to pay for anything.
- Make expectations about payment clear whether it is dinner or an airline ticket.
- Treat all your children with the same expectations in terms of financial assistance.
- Set your own limits about how far you are willing to go financially to support an adult child.
- If it is a specific event like a trip, explain what your budget is.
- Don't indulge your adult children by paying for their lifestyle when they cannot afford it themselves.
- Do things with your adult children that allow you to see them without any financial expense.

The Picker

As explained earlier, the picker leaves no stone unturned when visiting your home. His or her goal is to see what valuable goodies can be added to his or her own home. As the parents, you are usually on the losing end in this exchange because it is one way and the items are all leaving your house.

Obviously, there are probably some items that you would like to leave to your children. However all of your children need to be given an equal opportunity to choose these things. It should be left to the discretion of the parents as to when and where the items will leave, if at all. Here are some things to consider:

- Have estimates done by reputable estate liqui-dators to evaluate your belongings.
- Consider liquidating the items while you are still of sound mind.
- Place the names of children on specific items or list them in a will to indicate which items will be given to whom upon your death.
- Any item of value that is given to one child should be subtracted from the total value of the estate.
- Be discreet about the value of items, do not bring attention to something unnecessarily.
- Make it clear that no items are leaving your home with any of your children.
- Some valuables don't have to always be on display for children to see each time they visit.
- Remember that any item you give to one child without consulting with your other children could breed resentment.

The Squatter, Freeloader, Mr. or Ms. In-Between, Nowhere Man

As described, all of these individuals developed character traits early in their lives that should have been an early warning about dependency problems. Whether they are camped out in your house for the long haul, or are waiting for the next best thing, long-term they can be a pain in the ass.

These children prevent you from moving on with your life. As you plan to take more time for yourself, they will demand even more of your time and money. You are hostage to their inability to move on with their lives. It is important to be assertive with these children so they realize that you still have hopes and dreams yourself. And one of those dreams is for them to get out of your house now that they are in their thirties! These strategies might help:

- Just say no when they want to stay beyond their welcome.
- Don't renew your lease, so you can say that you have to move to a smaller place.
- If you own a home, list it with an agent claiming mounting, out-of-control expenses.
- Decrease or eliminate all services to them such as meals and clothes-washing.
- Charge rent. That's almost sure to scare them away.
- When they're not around rent their room out to boarders who will pay rent.
- Move to another city near other members of your family who are relatively independent.
- Calculate the rent they should have paid during the time they lived with you and remove it from their part of the total value of your estate. How and why you have done this should be clearly stipulated in your will.

The Sponge, the Neverlander and the Dreamer

The Sponge, the Neverlander and the Dreamer are similar—they are constantly hitting their parents up for more money, the only difference being the loftier misplaced ideas the dreamer has, and the cost. Regardless, these characters can be seen in both poor and wealthy families.

Usually parents of these children cannot anticipate what they are going to be asked for next, but they eventually begin to see the pattern. Usually they get a phone call and pleasantries are exchanged. The request is solicited: By the way, I just need…, and on it goes. The only thing left to figure out is how to avoid being the habitual target:

- Just say no.
- Consider call display features for your phone so you can screen your calls and not always answer calls.
- Do not keep much cash handy, and let them know.
- Make it clear that money is not loaned out until previous loans are repaid.
- Prepare a list of answers to ongoing requests for cash such as, I just got my tax bill and I have to pay that this month.
- If you can, get away for extended periods of time. It will probably save you money.

The Deadbeat

Your child who is also a deadbeat parent poses a particularly tough dilemma for any grandparent who is concerned about the well-being of their grandchildren. Often the responsibilities of parenthood have been shifted to grandparents over time because of neglect by the parents. The emotional

139

roller coaster that grandparents go through because of disappointment in their own child and genuine concern for their grandchild can make life both rewarding and miserable. The reward comes from providing for a grandchild in need while the misery comes from recognizing that your child is willing to do this to both you and his or her children.

The decision about how much you want to be involved must be coordinated with your spouse if you are married. Factors that need to be considered include your financial capabilities, space, and health. Without a doubt, the more you are involved, the less responsibility your child will take as a parent. The less you get involved the more at risk your grandchild is of being neglected. These tips can help you deal with this dilemma while allowing you to remain involved without creating a permanent dependency:

- Seek counselling for you and your spouse to discuss this situation.
- Seek counselling with your child to better understand why the neglect is happening.
- Recognize your child's limitations so you can make more objective decisions about providing assistance.
- Recognize your financial limitations about providing monetary support.
- Recognize your home limitations before providing room.
- Recognize your health limitations when considering providing a long-term parental role.
- Limit judgement statements against their parents because it will only confuse your grandchildren.
- Recognize when the emotional or financial strain

is too much.
- Accept the fact that you may not have the skills necessary to intervene to salvage the situation.
- Shouting matches between grandparents and parents will only further reduce the self-esteem of the grandchildren involved.
- Try not to let guilt consume you. Know when to back off if you can't take it any more because the situation is too overwhelming.

The Addict

It is disorienting to see the effect that an addiction can have on the child you raised. You often dwell on the memories of the child you knew because the person who confronts you now is impossible to understand. The addict is on a self-destruct path, and no matter how often you intervene, the scenarios rewind and play out over and over again.

An addict can place you in the most danger of becoming financially drained, regardless of the amount of money you have. Remember, for the addiction to be satisfied it must be fed, so whether the addiction is drugs, alcohol or gambling—family members, particularly parents, are dragged into the never-ending cycle of destructive behaviour. The need to feed the addiction is stronger than the need to please family members. Only with a firm commitment to kick the addiction, along with support by family and professionals, can this challenge be overcome. Remember that to help limit your vulnerability to this behaviour:

- Find out what you are actually dealing with in terms of the addiction and its effect on your child from books, Internet, etc....

- Seek counselling to understand how to deal with your son or daughter who has the addiction.
- An addiction can start at a young age, it is not restricted to adults.
- Contact an addiction rehabilitation centre to learn about treatment.
- As much as possible, avoid giving cash to your child.
- Do not lend out money until old debts have been repaid.
- Don't co-sign a loan.
- Do not leave cash lying around your home.
- Keep a close inventory of any valuables you have.
- Keep your purse or wallet out of sight when your child visits.
- Buy groceries for the addict before you give money for groceries.
- Be prepared to have an intervention with family and friends to persuade your child to go into a rehab centre.
- Remind your child that you love him or her and you want them to get help.
- Do not get into a shouting match with your son or daughter which might further alienate them, leaving you wondering where they are and what has happened to them.
- Keep close tabs on your financial health while attempting to hold off the needs of your addicted child.
- At some point you may have to finally decide to just say no.
- Contact the appropriate authorities if you feel threatened.

13. Conclusion

Because it is hard to say no, parents often find themselves in the situations I have described. Independence is a goal that all parents want their children to achieve. Sometimes there are difficulties that both parents and children have letting go when the time is right. The degree to which children slip into independence is the culmination of many factors that are a reflection of how they were raised and how parents perceive their care-giving role.

If parents always play the role of bank teller when their child makes demands, regardless of age, then that role will likely remain as the child ages. When a parent is consistently confronted by a child with unnecessary demands and repeatedly cannot muster up the courage to say no, then the demands will probably dramatically increase as the child moves into adulthood. It is easy to over-indulge any child once the line between what children need and what they want has become blurred.

Tantrums at a young age are an early form of manipulation which can change direction over your child's lifetime. Often parents become afraid or reluctant to deal with their demanding child's unwanted behaviours. For a while it seems easier to reach into a wallet and buy some peace but that only prolongs behaviours that become more difficult to deal with as the child ages. Opportunistic children who descend on their parents, like vultures in the desert, become far more threatening than the screaming child in the cashier line at the store. For many parents, the will to resist demands is replaced with a feeling of helplessness and resignation.

It is difficult for parents to comprehend the never-ending demands for funds and this is particularly true when the money is used for totally expendable goods and services. Hard-earned money is used for things that have little practical value, let alone long shelf life. The money is spent quickly on items that are rapidly outdated, creating a need to purchase even more unnecessary items. The cycle quickly escalates and only an observant and fast-acting parent can pull the plug on the bank machine before the machine runs out of cash.

O.P.M. (sounds like opium)

A friend of mine mentioned the term O.P.M. to me not long ago while we were discussing this book. He had heard some lawyers mention it when referring to people using Other Peoples' Money. What they were discussing was that, like the drug opium, O.P.M. can also become very addictive. Using Other Peoples' Money does little to help someone gain independence. Like the drug, using Other Peoples' Money can create a dependency that is difficult to kick.

By relying on others for financial support there is little need for ambition or motivation to find a career that will bring the financial rewards already being enjoyed.It is easy to delay dealing with reality while being encouraged to live in a fantasy. As long as a child is able to use Other Peoples' Money there is little incentive to rush out and try and find yourself.

The other thing about using Other Peoples' Money is that these children are not motivated to do any research about anything that they buy. They become big spenders and very poor consumers. There is little attempt to find the best deals because it makes no difference. When you are not using your own money, why bother developing consumer skills? The handicaps created by financial dependency keep multiplying.

The crazy thing is that the more money a parent has the more that parent is able to provide support. Ironically, the child who has been dependent into their adult years will one day inherit much of their parents' estate but be unable to manage the estate. Given the opportunity, the inheritance could be squandered much more swiftly than it took to accumulate. A ninety-year-old millionaire I knew became aware far too late that he was partially responsible for putting his fifty-five year old son in this position. He realized he could never leave his estate to his son without restrictions. After the old man died, the son had a yearly allotment that he could access while the other siblings received their share of the estate in full. The fifty-five year old couldn't manage any large sum of money even though he was a university graduate and, at one point, was a financial analyst for a large financial corporation. We are all susceptible.

Help Yourself and Your Child

It's never too late to take charge of the situation with your child. It is important to understand why you have allowed it get to such an extreme point. You can't ignore the factors motivating your child, regardless of age, to continually place financial demands on you. It is crucial to slow down the dynamic between child and parent to have time to respond differently, rather than simply fulfilling the request.

To do this you may have to prepare yourself for the

inevitable reaction to saying no to your child. Chances are that it will be difficult for you to do this, and you will feel far worse for much longer than any lingering effects it will have on your child. By proposing alternative solutions to always handing over money, you are encouraging your child to prepare for independence, regardless of his or her age— something worth far more than any amount of money you could possibly give.

A final point to consider: we celebrate our children's accomplishments all the time—and we must acknowledge the special things and not excessively praise mediocrity. Part of the special accomplishments your child achieves might be a reward you are comfortable providing. This is where the joy of being a proud parent able to provide gifts is so rewarding. There should be no guilt in providing for your child at appropriate times, when you can afford to do it. It is just as important that your child know how proud you are, as well as how meaningful the gift is, and how hard you had to work to provide it. When this happens, whatever you give serves its purpose. The event allows you to express your love with a token of appreciation for your child while allowing your child to raise his or her self-esteem and remain on a clear course toward independence.

Change is not easily achieved, particularly if you don't recognize your role in the dynamic that has been established with your child. Understanding the parental role you've established can be the catalyst you need to help you seriously consider alternative strategies that will help your child become financially independent. Change, whether incremental or dramatic, will have to be an ongoing obligation undertaken by parents to make a shift in a child's behaviour. This will allow our children to achieve personal independence in their lives.

Suggested Reading

A Parent's Guide to Money: Raising Financially Savvy Children, Alan Feigenbaum, Gibora Feigenbaum, Mars Publishing, 2002.

Grandparenthood, Ruth K. Westheimer, MacMillan Library, 1999.

How to Talk to Your Adult Children About Really Important Things, Theresa Foy DiGeronimo, John Wiley & Sons, Incorporated, 2001.

Launching Years: Strategies for Parenting from Senior Year to College Life, Laura Kastner, Jennifer Wyatt, Crown Publishing Group, 2002.

Parenting Teens with Love and Logic: Preparing Adolescents for Responsible Adulthood, Foster Cline, Jim Fay, NavPress Publishing Group, 2002.

Raising Financially Fit Kids, Joline Godfrey, Ten Speed Press, 2003.

Teenvestor: The Practical Investment Guide for Teens and Their Parents, Emmanuel Modu, Andrea Walker, Penguin, 2002.

The Parents Guide to Protecting Your Children in Cyberspace, Parry Aftab, McGraw-Hill Professional, 1999

When Grown Kids Disappoint Us: Letting Go of Their Problems, Loving Them Anyway, and Getting on with Our Lives, Jane Adams, Simon and Schuster, 2004.

Who's In Charge? A Guide to Family Management, Maggie Marmen, Creative Bound Incorporated, 2002.

Why Do they Act That Way? A Survival Guide to the Adolescent Brain for You and Your Teen, David Walsh PhD., Simon & Schuster Adult Publishing Group, 2005

You're on Your Own (But I'm Here If You Need Me): Mentoring Your child During the College Years, Marjorie Savage, Simon & Schuster Adult Publishing Group, July 2003

By the same author

DAD ALONE
How to Rebuild Your Life
and Remain an Involved Father
After Divorce

I Am Not an ATM Machine